THE AMERICAN DESIGNS
JENSEN SILVER

Nancy N. Schiffer and Janet Drucker
Photography by Douglas Congdon-Martin

4880 Lower Valley Road, Atglen, Pennsylvania 19310

Dedication

This work is dedicated to many years of effort by
Lolly Commanday (d. 2007)
to recognize, preserve, and understand the
American contributions to Georg Jensen Inc.
We acknowledge her vision and deeply miss her
passion, knowledge, and guidance.

Other Schiffer Books on Related Subjects:
Georg Jensen: A Tradition of Splendid Silver,
    Janet Drucker
Georg Jensen: 20th Century Designs,
    Preface by Janet Drucker
*Silver Jewelry Designs: Evaluating Quality
    Good * Better * Best*, Nancy Schiffer
Silver Jewelry Treasures, Nancy Schiffer

Copyright © 2008 by Janet Drucker and Schiffer Publishing Ltd.
Library of Congress Control Number: 2008920388

Designed by "Sue"
Type set in Zurich BT

ISBN: 978-0-7643-2738-4
Printed in China

Schiffer Books are available at special discounts for bulk purchases for sales promotions or premiums. Special editions, including personalized covers, corporate imprints, and excerpts can be created in large quantities for special needs. For more information contact the publisher:

Published by Schiffer Publishing Ltd.
4880 Lower Valley Road
Atglen, PA 19310
Phone: (610) 593-1777; Fax: (610) 593-2002
E-mail: Info@schifferbooks.com

For the largest selection of fine reference books on this and related subjects, please visit our web site at
www.schifferbooks.com
We are always looking for people to write books on new and related subjects. If you have an idea for a book please contact us at the above address.

This book may be purchased from the publisher.
Include $3.95 for shipping.
Please try your bookstore first.
You may write for a free catalog.

In Europe, Schiffer books are distributed by
Bushwood Books
6 Marksbury Ave.
Kew Gardens
Surrey TW9 4JF England
Phone: 44 (0) 20 8392-8585; Fax: 44 (0) 20 8392-9876
E-mail: info@bushwoodbooks.co.uk
Website: www.bushwoodbooks.co.uk
Free postage in the U.K., Europe; air mail at cost.

Acknowledgments

We appreciate the efforts of many people for their cooperation during the preparation of this book. Jewelry dealer Lolly Commanday, of Charlottsville, Virginia, was among the first to recognize good design in small articles of silver. She enthusiastically presented items for sale at "antique" shows throughout the eastern U. S. and would not let a potential customer leave her booth without making a strong pitch for her favorite designers. Lolly made a lasting impression on any would-be jewelry buyer with her humor, depth of knowledge, and passion—yes passion—for what she loved. She often clarified marks of little-known silversmiths and jewelers because their work was well know to her. She developed a highly focused interest and her retentive mind made connections between the makers and their individual styles, their use of decorative details, and their construction techniques. We owe a debt of gratitude to her and to others.

In particular, Chip deMatteo provided critical information on the work of his grandfather, William G. deMatteo, and we are sincerely grateful for his interest and support of our research. Chip provided photographs of William G. deMatteo's work and enabled Doug Congdon-Martin to take his pictures of Chip's family-owned items, original drawings, and supporting research materials. Doug also photographed the collections of the Robert Kaplon family as well as silver dealers Art Shea and Paul Smerker's extensive Romance With Silver collection of La Paglia's silver. They continue to be active promoters of his work.

Bill Drucker was very helpful in several phases of the work and found critical photographs that helped to visualize the story. Charles and Jennifer Phalon of Last Century Ltd. and Stephen Schreihman of Third Floor Antiques permitted items from their collections to be photographed and included. Ann Tradella kindly provided photographs of items sold by Skinner, Inc., auctioneers at Boston and Bolton, Massachusetts. Olivia Arnone, at The Newark Museum, sent an important photograph. Stanley J. Szaro, a fine silver dealer with Lauren Stanley American Silver in New York, took special interest in the book and provided photographs. Carmen Armstrong, of Adornments Unlimited in Houston, Texas, found unusual jewelry pieces by La Paglia and sent us photographs of them. We thank you all for advancing the story that we share here.

Preface

In the art world of paintings, an unsigned work with characteristics of a master painter, e.g. Matisse, Picasso, Cezanne, etc., can be described "after" or "in the style of" Matisse, Picasso, Cezanne, etc....The unsigned work, which exhibits similar characteristics to the "master" in style, technique, motif, etc., reveals significant qualities although they are not innumerated in the description. Visual recognition is sufficient.

Perhaps one can apply this analogy to the silverwork of makers, such as Alphonse La Paglia, William G. deMatteo, and others, that was made for the Georg Jensen Inc. store in New York between circa 1944 and 1951. At first glance, the viewer of a fully marked silver piece by La Paglia or deMatteo responds, "It's Jensen." A little hesitation, a re-evaluation, and "No, it isn't Jensen." This response is repeated often by the viewer and this reference is offered as a personal observation.

Contents

Chapter 1

Georg Jensen, Copenhagen, Denmark, and Georg Jensen Inc. U.S.A.

Georg Jensen and the Copenhagen, Denmark, Company

Danish silversmith Georg Jensen (1866-1935) opened a small workshop and retail store at 36 Bredgade in Copenhagen in 1904. Apprenticed to a goldsmith in 1880, Jensen had received training in drawing, perspective, and ceramics at a technical school and received his journeyman certificate as a goldsmith in 1884. His hope then was to become a sculptor, so he supported himself as a silversmith while he trained at the sculpture workshop of Professor Stein at the Royal Academy of Art in Copenhagen. In 1887, he was accepted as a sculpture student at the Royal Academy and completed his training in 1892. He married Marie Christiane Antoinette Wulff in 1891 and they had two sons, Vidar (b. 1891) and Jorgen (b. 1895). Tragically, Antoinette died in 1897, leaving Georg with the responsibility of raising his sons.

Georg enjoyed success as a sculptor and as a ceramist in the next few years, and tried several jobs in ceramics to earn a living. When he received a travel grant for work in ceramics, he embarked on a two-year tour of art centers in Europe in 1899. He met many artists and saw Art Nouveau masterpieces in Paris, and learned about the business side of art and met leading artists in applied arts in Italy and France. After he returned to Copenhagen in 1901, Georg Jensen found it difficult to raise a family on his earnings with ceramics, so he returned to his skill as a silversmith to finance his living. He worked with a number of Copenhagen silversmiths, including Mogens Ballin (1871-1914), who was a proponent of the Arts and Crafts movement in contemporary applied arts. Jensen began as a journeyman in Ballin's workshop and soon became the shop foreman. After success designing, creating, and selling silver items at the Ballin shop for three years, Georg Jensen decided to establish a workshop of his own. It opened on April 19, 1904. He was 38 years old.

The Georg Jensen silversmith business grew and gained fame quickly in Copenhagen, and won international recognition through exhibitions in other parts of Europe. In 1905 Jensen had a successful exhibit at the Folkwang Museum in Germany that traveled to various towns and introduced Jensen's work there. Jensen exhibited his work in 1909 at the Parisian galleries 'Salon d'Automne' and 'Art Décoratif', which became famous when its name was used to describe the new art style of the 1920s. Recognizing new markets outside Denmark, Danish art dealer Carl Dyhr proposed and opened a store in Berlin, Germany, in 1909, where Georg Jensen silver and Royal Copenhagen porcelain were sold. The success of this shop led to Germany becoming the Jensen firm's largest market until the First World War erupted in 1914.

Opposite page:
Champagne cooler, no. 87, made in the Georg Jensen A/S Copenhagen workshops, circa 1919. This was a wedding gift that Frederik Lunning presented to his daughter in 1945.

In 1910, Georg Jensen silver won a gold medal and international attention at the World Exhibition in Brussels, Belgium, and in 1913 Georg Jensen won the Diplôme d'Honneur award at the international exhibition in Ghent, Holland. The next year, Jensen silver was shown at the Baltic Exhibition in Mälmo, Sweden, where an art dealer from Stockholm, Nils Wendel, bought everything on display. Wendel continued to purchase and promote Georg Jensen silver in his gallery and later became Jensen's business partner. Swedish sales were gradually able to replace the loss of sales in the German market. A fuller description of the pre-World War One period in the company's history can be found in Janet Drucker's book, *Georg Jensen, A Tradition of Splendid Silver*.

The Georg Jensen company earned more widespread recognition when it was awarded gold medals at the Panama Pacific International Exposition in San Francisco, California, in 1915. Almost all of the Georg Jensen silver on display there was purchased by William Randolph Hearst, the newspaper owner and a leading art collector of the time.

Another retail shop was opened in Paris in 1918, at a fine location opposite the Place Vendôme on Rue St. Honoré. As the Georg Jensen Company grew to complete orders from the essential and growing retail markets, the workshop was relocated to a larger location in 1918, where it remained until 1988. Also in 1918, the Copenhagen retail sales shop was redesigned at great expense by Johan Rohde.

World War One brought devastating economic changes to Denmark and Europe. To address the continuing need for new retail markets after the war, a Georg Jensen store was opened in London in 1921. In 1935 the London shop was relocated to Bond Street, where it remains today.

Frederik Lunning and the New York Store

Frederik Lunning was a smart and ambitious book, music, paper, and art dealer at his shop, Lunnings Boghandel, at Overgade Nr. 9, in Odense, Denmark. On December 1, 1912, he ordered two women's hair combs from Georg Jensen in Copenhagen. The receipt is still extant (see *Georg Jensen, A Tradition in Splendid Silver,* page 46). Over the next few years, his success in selling Jensen silver to the public was noticed at the Jensen company. In 1918, therefore, Lunning was invited to become a salesman in the company's retail shop in Copenhagen. It was a good match, and Lunning grew in his work to become the manager of the store.

To develop the Danish market more fully, Frederik Lunning presented an exhibition of Jensen silver at the Danish palace Charlottenborg in 1920. Positive reviews by the Danish press and critics from abroad gave Jensen the acclaim they were seeking for the home market.

By 1921, an economic downturn in Denmark made the company finances unstable, and family members added personal funds to keep it afloat. Sales in London were unspectacular as well, not generating sales that had been hoped for. Lunning recalled the successful sale of silver exhibition pieces from the Panama Pacific Exhibition in San Francisco in 1915. He saw opportunity in the United States and proposed to develop a new market for the company there. With a lot of uncertainty, the company directors financed a venture by Lunning to the United States in 1922. He loaded trunks with Georg Jensen silver items and sailed on a ship to New York. There Lunning tried to interest retail stores like Tiffany and Company and Black, Star and Frost to take on the Jensen pieces, but they turned him down; the prices were too high, they explained.

Not willing to be discouraged, Frederik Lunning instead set up exhibits of the silver in elegant hotel surroundings and art galleries in New York. One was recalled: "an exhibition of Mr. Jensen's work was held in New York in 1922. The collection comprised of 400 specimens of his art and was shown at the Art Center, 65-67 East Fifty Sixth Street." (Obituary of Georg Jensen, *New York Times*, October 3, 1935) Two other exhibits are recorded at the Anderson Galleries at 489 Park Avenue, New York, one in December of 1923 and another in November of 1924. Emboldened with these successful efforts to sell Jensen silver in New York, Frederik Lunning became determined to open a Jensen store in the city.

He returned to Copenhagen to convince the company directors that his plans were sound. In the late 1920s, the directors granted Lunning rights to be the sole distributor of Jensen silver in the United States for 100 years. Lunning set up a new company to comply with this agreement and incorporated a business for himself as Georg Jensen Handmade Silver, Inc. He opened the first Jensen store in New York City at 159 West 57th Street in 1924.

Jensen silver was included in the "Danish National Exhibition of Applied Art, Painting, and Sculpture," that was on display at the Kunst und Industrie Museum in Copenhagen and then at the Brooklyn Museum in New York, in 1927. This was the first major Danish art exhibition to come to the United States, and it sparked long-lasting influence in America. The catalog for this exhibition states: "Georg Jensen has been the indisputable artistic leader of modern Danish silverware decoration and manufacture. Happily combining the personality and attainments of artists and craftsmen, he has executed a series of works, partly of his own designs, partly after the designs of eminent painter Johan Rohde, and the technique of his works, their simple forms and characteristic open work ornamentation, have spread his fame throughout Europe and America." In a review of the exhibition for the *New York Times*, art critic Elizabeth L. Cary suggested that the Danish tradition of using talents of the nation's top artists to elevate the design of manufactured goods was a model worth emulating in the United States. The Brooklyn Museum's exhibition helped to establish the high reputation of Jensen silver in America.

And the Brooklyn Museum was not alone in its high regard for Georg Jensen silver. The Newark (New Jersey) Museum purchased Jensen silver jewelry and hollowware for their permanent collections in November of 1929. The original bill of sale remains in the museum archives for two necklaces, an ashtray, and a Johan Rohde-designed pitcher.

The following year, 1930, the Museum of Fine Arts in Boston, Massachusetts, organized The American Federation of Arts Exhibition of Decorative Metalwork and Cotton Textiles, The Third International Exhibition of Contemporary Industrial Art. Displayed were contemporary industrial arts from Czechoslovakia, Denmark, England, France, Germany, Holland, Sweden, Switzerland, and the United States. After its venue in Boston, the exhibits traveled on to The Metropolitan Museum of Art in New York, The Art Institute of Chicago in Chicago, Illinois,

Compote with grape design, no. 263A, made by Georg Jensen and bearing the early GJ mark, c. 1928. 5" x 5". Engraved, "Presented to Frederik Lunning with thanks for 10 years of service, A/S Georg Jensen & Wendel." It was given to Lunning in 1928.

The emblem in silver for the New York store of Georg Jensen, Inc. at 667 Fifth Avenue from 1935 to 1970

The building at 667 Fifth Avenue, New York, where the Georg Jensen shop was located, c. mid-1940s

The front window and door of the 667 Fifth Avenue, New York, shop of Georg Jensen, Inc., c. mid-1940s.

Interior of the New York shop of Georg Jensen, Inc. at 667 Fifth Avenue, showing the variety of luxury goods displayed on the shelves and Frederik Lunning standing with the customers, c. mid-1940s.

and The Cleveland Museum of Art in Cleveland, Ohio. George Jensen exhibited ten objects in silver, including bowls, boxes, candlesticks, cocktail shakers, cups, tea sets, and vases. Three entries were labeled "Courtesy of Georg Jensen Handmade Silver, New York," indicating Frederik Lunning's continuing efforts to present Jensen silver among the leading artistic goods in the world. An advertisement printed in the *International Studio* publication of April, 1931, lists the address for his company at "169 West 57th Street, New York City, opposite Carnegie Hall."

Frederik Lunning was busy growing his business and international appreciation for Jensen silver. He moved the New York shop in 1935 to a new and even better location, at 667 Fifth Avenue near 53rd Street, for marketing to his uptown clientele.

By this time, the products of the Copenhagen company Georg Jensen had reached international acclaim, and they must have brought confident pride to its founder. When he unfortunately died on October 2, 1935, George Jensen was described in the *New York Times* obituary as "the greatest craftsman in silver for the last 300 years." His obituary in the London *Times* concluded that, "Jensen is one of those craftsmen whose pieces can safely be regarded as antiques of the future." That prediction has become reality.

After the founder of Georg Jensen silver died, the company continued with directors and family members maintaining the craftsmanship traditions and standards laid out by the master before them. The workshops continued to fill orders that came in from the retail shops and to create new items of artistic merit.

The 1939 New York World's Fair provided another opportunity to display Georg Jensen silver in an international setting. In the Pavilion of Nations, outstanding creations of art and industry from Denmark were featured. The official guidebook stated, "Except for world famous porcelain, silverware and other Danish art craft, no commercial products are exhibited." But there, Frederik Lunning's Georg Jensen store of New York and the Royal Copenhagen Company exhibited handmade silver jewelry and silverware, porcelain, stoneware, crystal wooden toys, and objects of pewter and bronze. Therefore, the thousands of international fair visitors were exposed to the modern Danish designs and the Jensen silver items on display.

The popularity of modern Danish designs was growing in America far beyond the retail center of New York City. The L. & C. Mayers Company, which started in 1912, had a thriving mail order business in jewelry, household items, and gifts with showrooms for the public at two locations in New York City, also Albany and Buffalo, New York; Philadelphia, Pennsylvania; and Hartford, Connecticut. Their catalogs were sent throughout the country. The 1939 L. & C. Mayers Company catalog features a full-page illustrated display of "Sterling Silver Jewelry, beautifully Made Pins and Bracelets. Patterned from Authentic Danish Designs. Good Weight. Finished by Hand." Each of the designs shown resembles a Georg Jensen design. They were apparently manufactured in quantity and hand-finished. Their place of manufacture is not disclosed in the catalog. Clearly, more and more Americans were being exposed to good Danish designs before 1940.

STERLING SILVER JEWELRY

Beautifully Made Pins and Bracelets. Patterned from Authentic Danish Designs. Good Weight. Finished by Hand. Pins have Safety Catches; Bracelets Safety Chains. Neat Gift Boxes. Illustrations Actual Size.

Prices Subject to Catalog Discounts. See Page 1.

AJ2386 Sterling Silver Pin $5.50
Bird and Cherry motif. Bright finish, good weight. Embossed and pierced design. Safety catch.

AJ2387 Sterling Silver Pin $3.70
Violet motif. Bright finish, good weight. Embossed and pierced design. Safety catch.

AJ2388 Sterling Silver Pin $3.40
Dove and Foliage motif. Bright finish, good weight. Embossed and pierced design. Safety catch.

AJ2389 Sterling Silver Pin $6.50
Leaf and Blossom motif. Bright finish, good weight. Embossed and pierced design. Safety catch.

AJ2390 Sterling Silver Pin $6.00
Dove and Oak Leaf motif. Bright finish, good weight. Embossed and pierced design. Safety catch.

AJ2391 Sterling Silver Pin $6.50
Leaf and Blossom motif. Bright finish, good weight. Embossed and pierced design. Safety catch.

AJ2392 Sterling Silver Pin............. $7.00
Faun and Foliage motif. Bright finish, good weight. Embossed and pierced design. Safety catch.

AJ2393 Sterling Silver Bracelet $6.70
Leaf and Berry motif. Bright finish, good weight. Embossed and pierced design. Secure clasp and safety chain.

AJ2394 Sterling Silver Bracelet.. $9.80
Leaf and Blossom motif. Bright finish, good weight. Embossed and pierced design. Secure clasp and safety chain.

AJ2395 Sterling Silver Bracelet.. $12.20
Dove and Foliage motif. Bright finish, good weight. Embossed and pierced design. Secure clasp and safety chain. Effectively matches pins AJ2388 and AJ2390.

L. & C. MAYERS CO. FIFTH AVE., NEW YORK

III

A page from the L. & C. Mayers Co. catalog for 1939, showing Danish-inspired jewelry being offered in the United States.

Chapter 2

American Silversmith/Designers

The luxury goods market was thriving in America in the early 20th century. Artists and master craftsmen provided affluent people with high quality domestic furnishings in urban areas throughout the country. In New York City in particular, competition was strong for contracts to furnish elegant homes with superior quality goods, including silver forms. When Frederik Lunning sought craftsmen with whom to work for his store in the early 1940s, he had many choices from which to pick. Records indicate there were other silversmiths he worked with and items of Jensen Inc. silver bear a variety of makers' marks, including "Jo Pol" (whose mark was Jo Pol, identity unknown) and Lawrence Foss (whose mark was L/F in an oval). Also, there were other makers listed in a 1947 catalog (see Chapter 3). Most prominent among the American silversmiths were William G. deMatteo and Alphonse La Paglia, for whom relatively abundant items remain and information has come forth. Perhaps others of the makers can be identified and recognized in the future.

William G. deMatteo

Gaetano deMatteo (1895-1981) was born in the tiny fishing village of Acciaroli, in the province of Salerno, Italy, on March 17, 1895. His father, Luciano, and all the men in his family before him, were fishermen. Sixty years later, Ernest Hemingway would be inspired by the fishermen of Acciaroli to write his epic book, *The Old Man and The Sea*. Luciano immigrated to New York around 1898 and became a United States citizen. He returned to Italy in 1905 and brought 10-year-old Gaetano back to New York with him. The son's immigration papers at Ellis Island, New York, mysteriously had the name William added, and from that time forward he was known as William G. deMatteo.

As a boy, William had claimed a desire to become a doctor, but his formal education ended when he arrived in America. After an assortment of menial jobs by the age of fourteen, in 1909, he was employed to sweep the floors at the silversmith Reed & Barton's Fifth Avenue workshop. Someone took a liking to him and he was quickly made an apprentice; in five years he became a journeyman. William was probably the youngest person to be a silversmith and then foreman at the shop.

In 1917, deMatteo married Elizabeth, and during their 64-year marriage they had two children: Margaret, born in 1920, and William L. "Bill", born in 1923. In 1921, at age twenty six, deMatteo opened his own shop in New York City. Little is known about this period, although family members suggest that he supported his family by doing silver repair work. He built a small house in 1926, at 53 Harcourt Avenue in

William G. deMatteo raising a silver bowl, c. 1950. *Courtesy of Chip deMatteo*

Bergenfield, New Jersey, a close suburban community to New York. Behind the house he built a small shop, which remained his workshop until his retirement. He marked the items he made with a capital D in a circle or with his name in capital block letters DEMATTEO and with the words in capital letters HAND HAMMERED or HAND MADE.

According to his grandson, Chip deMatteo, William G. deMatteo "was not a large man and he was probably even smaller as a boy when he learned to raise and planish at Reed & Barton. He was taught to hammer as most silversmiths do, towards their body, but found because of his size, that there was more mechanical advantage hammering away from his body, like a carpenter driving a nail. He used this "backwards" technique his whole life."

DeMatteo built a stable clientele for his silver business by designing and making items for the carriage trade in New York City. He was eager to assimilate into the American middle class. He enjoyed nice cars and loved to garden, which yielded him prize-winning dahlias. His garden wheelbarrow, which he could see from his workshop, inspired him to make a silver replica, a perfect miniature reproduction, which he later donated to The Newark Museum, in New Jersey.

DeMatteo's customer list was comprised of the elite of Manhattan's finest retailers that dealt in silver hollowware. In the early years, he took commissions, making specific pieces requested by his customers. These included reproductions of colonial-style bowls and pitchers for S. Wyler and Shrubsole.

The 1930s depression years dampened New York's economy, causing deMatteo's business to slump a little. He was well established by then, and his business had low overhead. In fact, he suffered far less than many of his friends and neighbors who had worked in business in New York and became unemployed.

When deMatteo had an overload of business, he often hired help, none of which lasted for any length of time. During the early years of the depression there was no need for extra hands in the shop. But during the later thirties, he invoked a secret weapon, his son William L. "Bill" deMatteo, who was then old enough to work in the shop. DeMatteo built a wooden box for Bill to stand on at the workbench and set out to teach him all he could about the trade. As his new helper grew, business improved and the extra pair of hands was rewarded with more orders. deMatteo was producing commissioned special orders for his customers, including Tiffany & Company and Cartier in New York.

On the floor of deMatteo's workshop, he painted a line that was a measured distance from a shelf on the wall. The line represented the distance from the curb to the window at Tiffany & Company on Fifth

Marks used by William G. deMatteo. *Courtesy of Chip deMatteo*

Miniature Wheelbarrow
William G. de Matteo, New Jersey, ca. 1947
Silver
Gift of Mr. William G. De Matteo, 1975
Collection of The Newark Museum

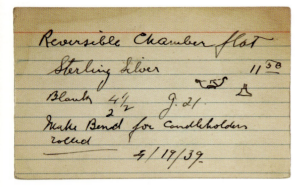

William G. deMatteo's record card for a Reversible Chamber pot (?), dated 4/19/39. *Courtesy of Chip deMatteo*

Small footed bowl with a beaded rim, made by William G. deMatteo. *Courtesy of Chip deMatteo*

Avenue. He would inspect every piece at this distance to see that the pieces had balance and flow. When he was satisfied, he would declare the item "O.K. for Fifth Avenue."

Business was steady and life was good for the deMatteo family. As a teenager, Bill improved his skills until he was a fully qualified silversmith in his own right. However, during World War II, Bill joined the U. S. Navy, fulfilling his desire to fly airplanes. Losing his captive helper was difficult for the elder deMatteo, at a time when the shop was very busy with work.

To work out the designs of his silver items, William G. deMatteo kept drawings of his ideas on index cards in his workshop until the mid-1940s. Some are preserved by his family and reveal his decisions in calculating the sizes and proportions of the finished items. From about 1945 to 1948, he kept his designs in a bound book. They reflect his orders for private commissions as well as for Georg Jensen Inc. The Jensen-inspired items in deMatteo's design book run the gamut from nearly identical reproductions of Jensen designs, as in his number 46 tea and coffee service that is almost indistinguishable from Jensen's famous No. 2 service, to wholly original designs in the Jensen style. Where they are relevant to the items that appear in this book, deMatteo's drawings are shown with his finished items.

The events of World War II significantly impacted silver imports from Denmark, as has been described in Chapter 1. As a result, Frederik Lunning, as owner of Georg Jensen Inc., commissioned William G. deMatteo and other silversmiths to produce for his shop silver items that were in the style of Georg Jensen's designs. DeMatteo easily adapted to the Danish designs and developed similar hollowware, with tendrils and blossoms close enough to resemble Georg Jensen's singular style. Over the period of about 1944 to 1951, deMatteo made thousands of pieces in a few hundred designs in the Jensen style for sale at the New York store and through its catalogs.

William G. deMatteo continued to make these and similar designs until he retired, and they represent his best-known work. As late as 1974, there were old stock deMatteo-made fluted compotes for sale in the Georg Jensen Inc. store in Manhattan, as observed by a family member who recalled the specific details of deMatteo's earlier designs. The items were fully marked by the silversmith.

Two footed bowls made by William G. deMatteo. *Courtesy of Chip deMatteo*

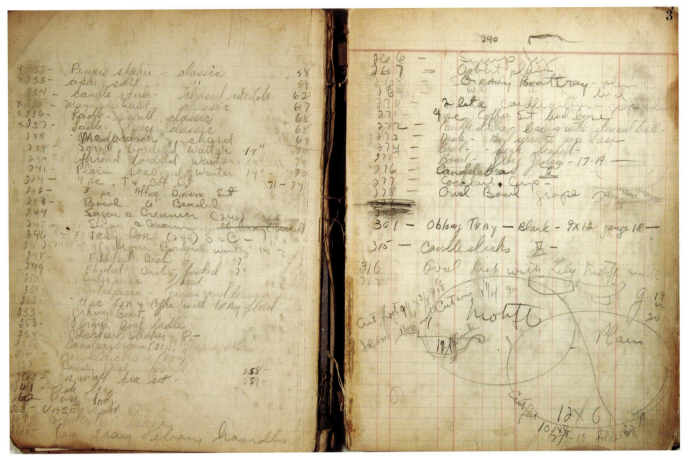

William G. deMatteo's design records book, pages 2 and 3, descriptions for item numbers 236 to 316. *Courtesy of Chip deMatteo*

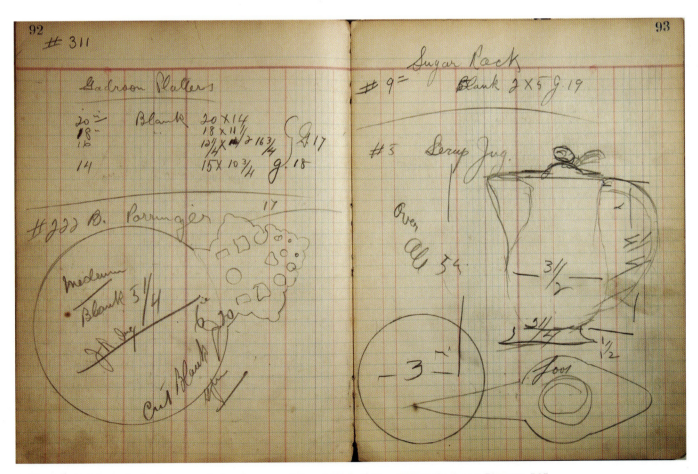

William G. deMatteo's design records book, pages 92 and 93. Left Top, "#311 Gadroon Platters, 20" Blank 20x14 g.17, 18" 18x11 ½, 16 12 1/4x16 ¾, 14 14x10 ¾ g.18." Left Bottom, "#222 B. Porringer, Medium, Blank 5 ¼, JR Ivy, Cut Blank" Right Top, "Sugar Rack #9 – Blank 2x5 g19." Right Bottom, #5 Syrup Jug, overall 5", foot." *Courtesy of Chip deMatteo*

Bowl with spun foot made by William G. deMatteo, 7" diameter x 4 ½" high. *Courtesy of Chip deMatteo*

William G. deMatteo's record card for Scallop Bowl No. 12, in 12 sections. *Courtesy of Chip deMatteo*

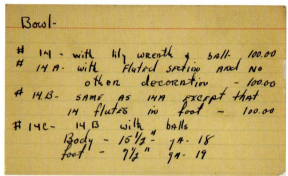

William G. deMatteo's record card for Bowls #14, #14A, #14B, and #14C. *Courtesy of Chip deMatteo*

Footed, scalloped bowl #14 made by William G. deMatteo. *Courtesy of Chip deMatteo*

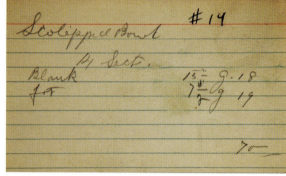

William G. deMatteo's record card for [Scalloped] Bowl #14. *Courtesy of Chip deMatteo*

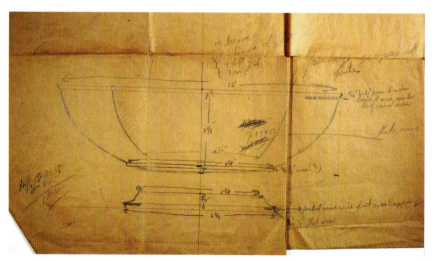

William G. deMatteo's design for a bowl. *Courtesy of Chip deMatteo*

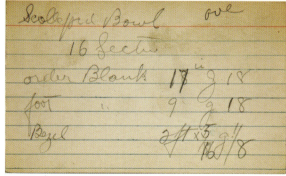

William G. deMatteo's record card for a Scalloped Bowl of 16 sections. *Courtesy of Chip deMatteo*

Gravy boat made by William G. deMatteo, 7" wide x 3 ½" high. *Courtesy of Chip deMatteo*

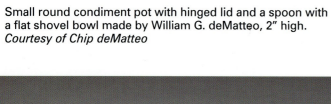

Small round condiment pot with hinged lid and a spoon with a flat shovel bowl made by William G. deMatteo, 2" high. *Courtesy of Chip deMatteo*

Large pap boat (ash tray) made by William G. deMatteo, 7" long. *Courtesy of Chip deMatteo*

Pap boat made by William G. deMatteo, 5" high. *Courtesy of Chip deMatteo*

Pair of salt and pepper shakers #107 made by William G. deMatteo, 5" high. *Courtesy of Chip deMatteo*

Pair of Chippendale style candlesticks made by William G. deMatteo, 7" high. *Courtesy of Chip deMatteo*

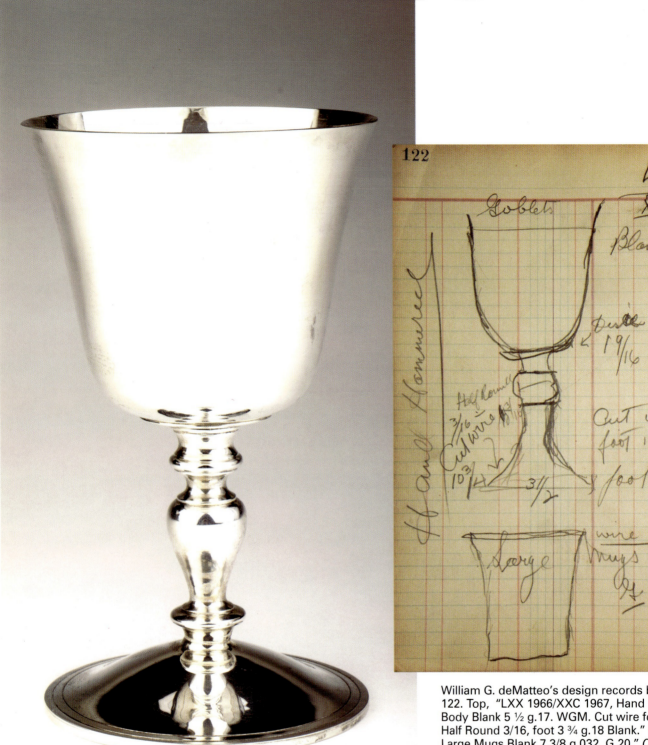

William G. deMatteo's design records book, page 122. Top, "LXX 1966/XXC 1967, Hand Hammered, Body Blank 5 ½ g.17. WGM. Cut wire for foot 10 ¾- Half Round 3/16, foot 3 ¾ g.18 Blank." Bottom, "wire, Large Mugs Blank 7 3/8 g.032, G 20." *Courtesy of Chip deMatteo*

Goblet made by William G. deMatteo, 7" high. *Courtesy of Chip deMatteo*

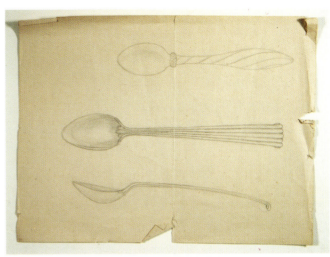

Pair of long-handled serving spoons made by William G. deMatteo, 13" long. *Courtesy of Chip deMatteo*

William G. deMatteo's design for spoons. *Courtesy of Chip deMatteo*

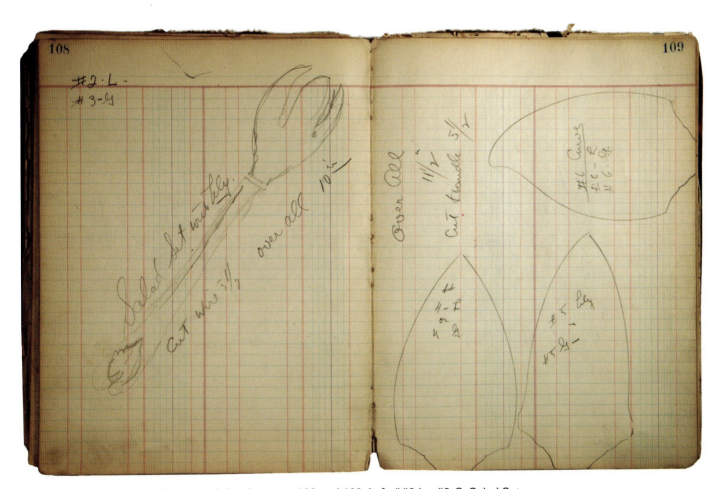

William G. deMatteo's design records book, pages 108 and 109. Left, "#2-L-, #3-G. Salad Set with Lily, Cut Wire 5 1/2 , overall 10 in." Right, "#6 Curve, Over all 11 ½, Cut Handle 5 ½, #4-L or 4 G. #5 Lily- #5 G-." *Courtesy of Chip deMatteo*

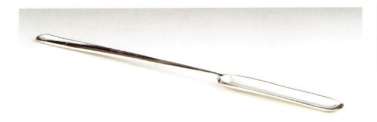

Marrow scoop made by William G. deMatteo, 10" long. *Courtesy of Chip deMatteo*

Candle snuffer with ring handle made by William G. deMatteo, 10" long. *Courtesy of Chip deMatteo*

Sauce boat made by William G. deMatteo. *Courtesy of Chip deMatteo*

Small gravy boat made by William G. deMatteo. *Courtesy of Chip deMatteo*

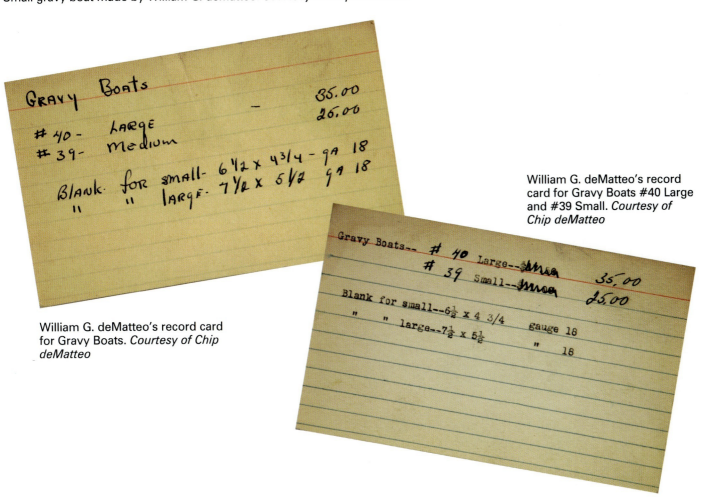

William G. deMatteo's record card for Gravy Boats #40 Large and #39 Small. *Courtesy of Chip deMatteo*

William G. deMatteo's record card for Gravy Boats. *Courtesy of Chip deMatteo*

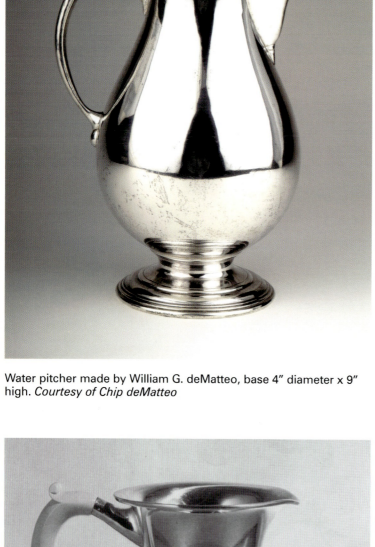

Water pitcher made by William G. deMatteo, base 4" diameter x 9" high. *Courtesy of Chip deMatteo*

Water pitcher made by William G. deMatteo. *Courtesy of Chip deMatteo*

William G. deMatteo's record card for #11 Water Pitcher [with] Ivory Handle. *Courtesy of Chip deMatteo*

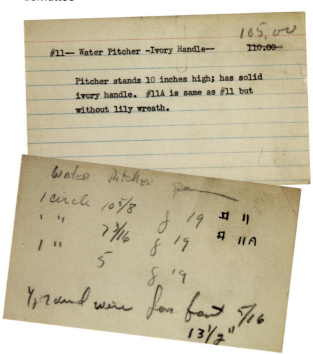

William G. deMatteo's record card for Water Pitcher #11. *Courtesy of Chip deMatteo*

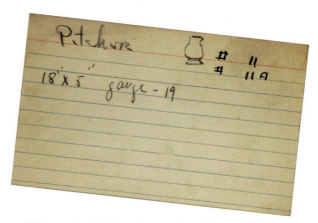

William G. deMatteo's record card for Pitcher #11. *Courtesy of Chip deMatteo*

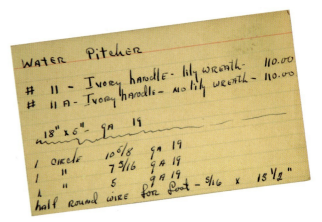

William G. deMatteo's record card for Water Pitchers #11 and #11A, with ivory handles. *Courtesy of Chip deMatteo*

Cream pitcher with a cast handle, made by William G. deMatteo, 5" high. *Courtesy of Chip deMatteo*

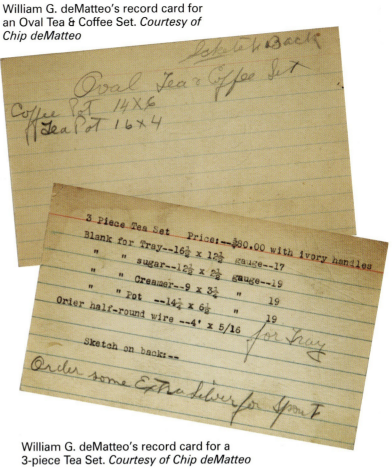

William G. deMatteo's record card for an Oval Tea & Coffee Set. *Courtesy of Chip deMatteo*

William G. deMatteo's record card for a 3-piece Tea Set. *Courtesy of Chip deMatteo*

4-piece tea set #250 made by William G. deMatteo. *Courtesy of Chip deMatteo*

3-piece coffee set #15 made by William G. deMatteo.

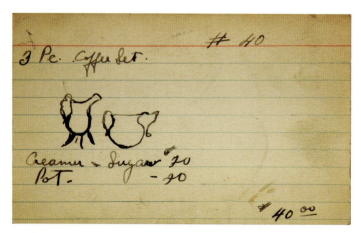

William G. deMatteo's record card for #40, 3-piece Coffee Set.
Courtesy of Chip deMatteo

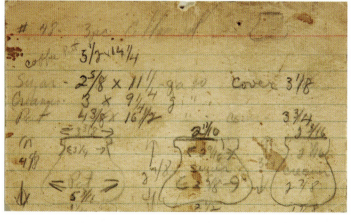

William G. deMatteo's record card for #48, 3-piece Coffee Set.
Courtesy of Chip deMatteo

Large conical coffee pot with ebony handle, made by William G. deMatteo, 14" high. *Courtesy of Chip deMatteo*

William G. deMatteo's design records book, pages 119 and 121. Left, "Cover, Regular Pot. Base 7" inside, WB/Dmatteo." *Courtesy of Chip deMatteo*

William G. deMatteo's record card for a Sugar [bowl and cream pitcher]. *Courtesy of Chip deMatteo*

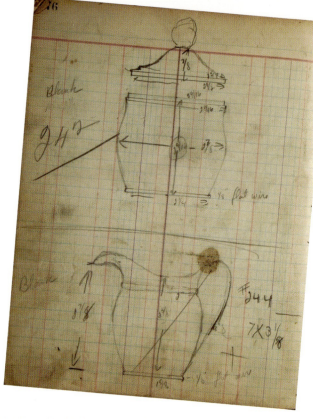

William G. deMatteo's design records book, page 76. Blank, #242 [covered barrel shape]. Blank [pitcher] #244 → [bottom of right page] Sugar Jar #244 is same as 242- page 82- without cover-." *Courtesy of Chip deMatteo*

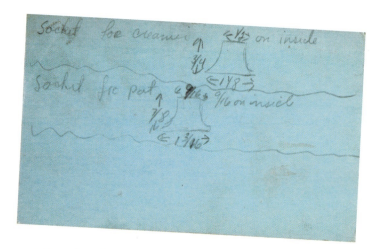

William G. deMatteo's record card for sockets for a creamer and a pot. *Courtesy of Chip deMatteo*

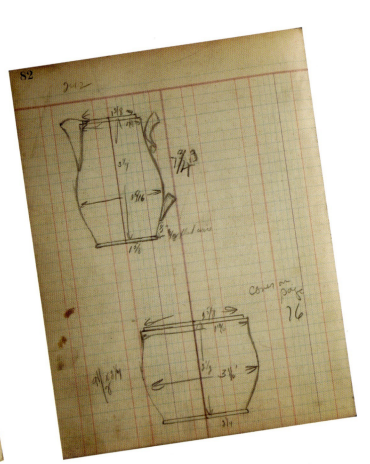

William G. deMatteo's design records book, page 82. Top, "242- ½ flat wire." Left Bottom, "Cover on page 76." *Courtesy of Chip deMatteo*

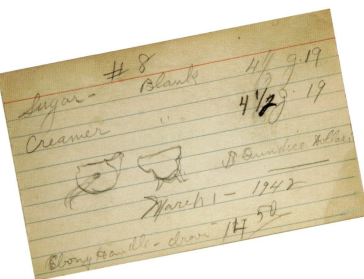

William G. deMatteo's record card for #8 Sugar [bowl] and Creamer, dated March 1-1942. *Courtesy of Chip deMatteo*

William G. deMatteo annealing a sterling item in his workshop.

Oval tray with a beaded border, made by William G. deMatteo

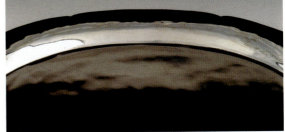

Flat card tray made by William G. deMatteo, 8" long x 5" wide. *Courtesy of Chip deMatteo*

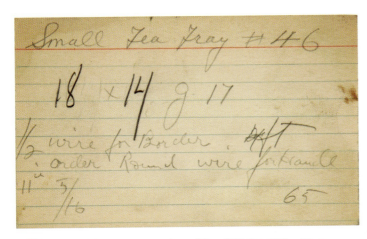

William G. deMatteo's record card for #46 Small Tea Tray. *Courtesy of Chip deMatteo*

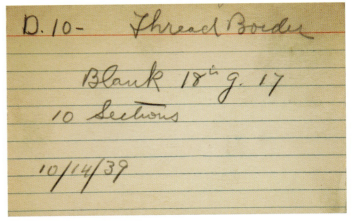

William G. deMatteo's record card for D-10 Thread Border [tray], dated 10/14/39. *Courtesy of Chip deMatteo*

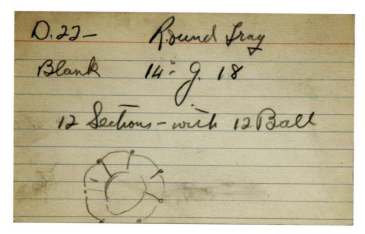

William G. deMatteo's record card for D.22- Round Tray. *Courtesy of Chip deMatteo*

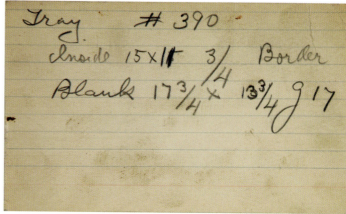

William G. deMatteo's record card for #390 Tray. *Courtesy of Chip deMatteo*

Round footed tray made by William G. deMatteo, 7" diameter. *Courtesy of Chip deMatteo*

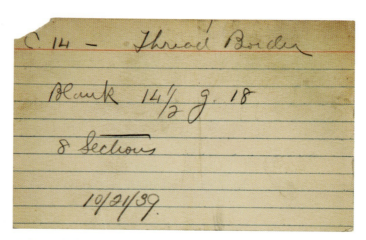

William G. deMatteo's record card for [#]14 Thread Border [tray] of 8 sections, dated 10/21/[19]39. *Courtesy of Chip deMatteo*

Scalloped-edge waiter #247 made by William G. deMatteo. *Courtesy of Chip deMatteo*

Large footed tray with shell border and claw feet made by William G. deMatteo, 13"
diameter. *Courtesy of Chip deMatteo*

William G. deMatteo's record card for a Gadroon Waiter, dated
January 21/[19]43. *Courtesy of Chip deMatteo*

William G. deMatteo soldering a tray border. *Courtesy of Chip deMatteo*

Miniature flat card tray made by William G. deMatteo, 4" long x 2 ½" wide. *Courtesy of Chip deMatteo*

Small round tray with a bud, made by William G. deMatteo, 3 ½" diameter. *Courtesy of Chip deMatteo*

Alphonse LaPaglia

Alphonse La Paglia was contracted by Frederik Lunning to create designs for jewelry and hollowware specifically in the Jensen style. La Paglia was a master craftsman who created unique interpretations of Jensen motifs. For example, La Paglia used the blossom, magnolia, acorn, and silver leaves in his compositions. The familiar motifs were reworked and produced in sterling silver with an open back, as opposed to the traditional closed backs of Georg Jensen.

Each piece of Alphonse La Paglia's jewelry and hollowware has his unique identifying marks, which include his product numbers, and these numbers had no relation to the product design numbers of Georg Jensen A/S of Copenhagen. La Paglia's initials "LP" appear often on his work, as well as his "straw" mark. In Italian, the word for "straw" is "LAPOLLIA." This mark is a bundle of wheat sheaves with his initials, L and P, on either side of the bundle and within a shaped cartouche. A variation of his mark is his full name in script or "ALP." The work La Paglia did for Lunning's New York shop include the mark "Georg Jensen Inc., U.S.A." (see Chapter 3).

We assume that La Paglia worked for Frederik Lunning until about 1948 to 1951. The Georg Jensen Company in Denmark took issue with Lunning's production of silver items in America at about this time.

Alphonse La Paglia in his silver workshop, c. 1952, on the cover of *Silver Magazine*, May/June, 1995.

Pair of #114 console bowls made by Alphonse La Paglia, small, 3.75 x 5.
Courtesy of Dr. Morton & Maidie Kaplon of Summit, New Jersey

Console bowl #118 made by Alphonse La Paglia. 5.75" x 10". *Courtesy of Romance with Silver Collection*

A 3-arm pedestal candlestick made by Alphonse La Paglia.

Two 2-arm candelabras #121 made by
Alphonse La Paglia. 7 5/8" wide x 10" high.
Courtesy of Romance with Silver Collection

Jam jar #205 made by Alphonse La Paglia (block letters), original glass, leaf finial, 4 ¼".
Courtesy of Romance with Silver Collection

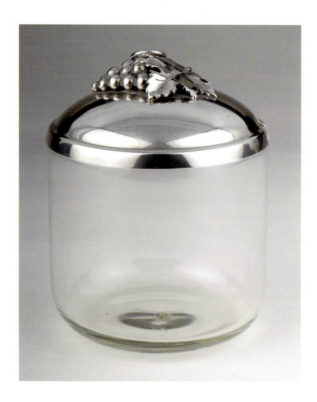

Jam jar #205, in the grape pattern, with original glass body and grapes finial, made by Alphonse La Paglia (with block letters mark), 4" high. *Courtesy of Romance with Silver Collection*

Covered bonbon dish #108, made by Alphonse La Paglia. 3.5" tall x 5 .25" x 3.75". *Courtesy of Dr. Morton & Maidie Kaplon of Summit, New Jersey*

Trumpet flute #1170 34/4, with an unusual marking, possibly made by Alphonse La Paglia. 3 7/8" diameter, 5 ¼" high. Part of a boxed set. *Courtesy of Romance with Silver Collection*

Covered serving dish made by Alphonse La Paglia. *Courtesy of Skinner Inc., Boston and Bolton, Massachusetts*

Small covered box #123, made by Alphonse La Paglia, 4 1/8" x 3" x 2 ½" high. *Courtesy of Romance with Silver Collection*

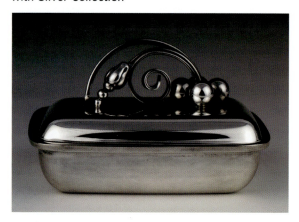

Vegetable dish #112, made by Alphonse La Paglia, 11 ¾" x 7 1/8" x 2 ½" high. *Courtesy of Romance with Silver Collection*

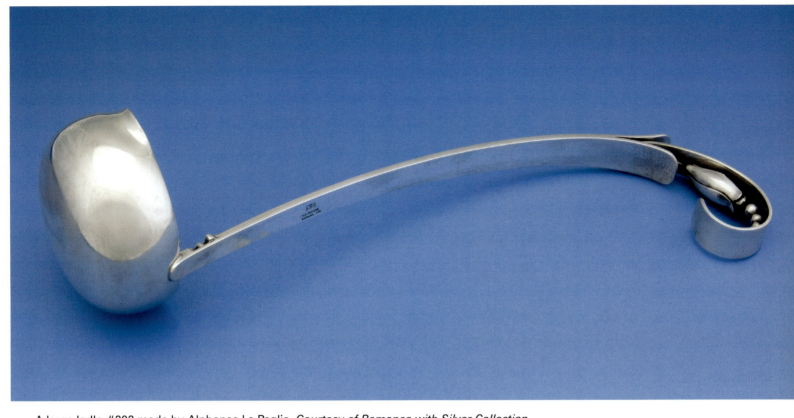

A large ladle #202 made by Alphonse La Paglia. *Courtesy of Romance with Silver Collection*

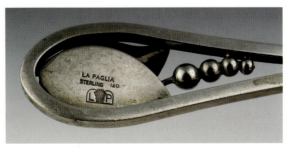

Coaster #123 made by Alphonse La Paglia (with the block letters mark), 4" wide. *Courtesy of Romance with Silver Collection*

Cake server #120 made by Alphonse La Paglia (block letters mark), 11 ½" long. *Courtesy of Romance with Silver Collection*

Small ladle #205 made by Alphonse La Paglia (block letters mark), 5" long. *Courtesy of Romance with Silver Collection*

Set of four goblets #205 made by Alphonse La Paglia, 6 ¼" high x 3 ½" diameter. *Courtesy of Romance with Silver Collection*

Five demitasse spoons made by Alphonse La Paglia, 4" long. *Courtesy of Dr. Morton & Maidie Kaplon of Summit, New Jersey.*

Letter opener #204 made by Alphonse La Paglia, 10 ¼" long. *Courtesy of Romance with Silver Collection*

Two napkin rings with a pierced floral band, made by Alphonse La Paglia. *Courtesy of Romance with Silver Collection*

Salt and pepper shakers, with a gilded lining on the salt shaker, made by Alphonse La Paglia, 4.75" high. *Courtesy of Romance with Silver Collection*

A 5-piece tea service containing 228 ounces of silver, made by Alphonse La Paglia. *Courtesy of Skinner Inc., Boston and Bolton, Massachusetts*

A 4-piece tea service including a teapot engraved P, a cream pitcher, a covered sugar bowl, and a rectangular tray, each made by Alphonse La Paglia. *Courtesy of Skinner Inc., Boston and Bolton, Massachusetts*

Link bracelet of five scrolled leaf and blossom design links, marked by La Paglia for George Jensen Inc. U.S.A., Sterling. *Courtesy of Carmen Armstrong, Adornments Unlimited*

Chapter 3

American Silver Designs for Georg Jensen Inc. U.S.A.

Frederik Lunning's Georg Jensen Inc. store in New York City was the center of American distribution for Georg Jensen A/S silver items by 1939. Lunning had worked effectively and tirelessly for fifteen years to raise public awareness for Georg Jensen silver in America and to provide many orders for fulfillment at the workshops in Copenhagen.

Political events in Europe evolved by 1939 into the beginnings of World War Two. As the war developed, silver became unavailable for commercial use, and the production of Jensen items in Copenhagen became limited. The transportation of goods across the Atlantic Ocean became dangerous and unpredictable, because of submarine warfare. Unable to fill his orders and his shelves with Copenhagen-derived Georg Jensen items, Frederik Lunning was forced to augment his inventory with goods he could obtain in America. Lunning brought to his shop goods that were commissioned from American sources about 1940.

America moved into the shop. Everything— literally everything could now be sold. From being an exclusive silver and china shop, which he was able to survey with his strategic eye, the firm turned into a much bigger, but also much more confused three-storied mixed shop— with 300 employees and 3,000 problems! (*The Lunning Prize*, p. 12)

Designs by William G. deMatteo

The American-made sterling silver that was sold at the Georg Jensen Inc. store in New York was not made exactly to match Jensen silver of Copenhagen, but each piece has its own personality and is easily identified by the Georg Jensen Inc., U.S.A. mark.

DeMatteo's take on Jensen's No. 264 compote provides an interesting insight into deMatteo's methods and a contrast with the Georg Jensen factory operation. DeMatteo's compote number 69 was made in at least a dozen variations, probably many more. All of them share the same seven-inch flared bowl, approximately two inches deep. They are all seven inches tall. Most of them have a similar 3 1/3 inch base. The base and bowl were hand-raised and planished in small batches, usually from guage 18 stock. The cross-section of the bases varies, the curve of which needed to match the width of the bottom of the stem, which often varied in dimension. Most of the compotes had beaded wire trimming at the bottom and top of the base where it meets the stem, some did not, and still others had various round galleries, sometimes with a detail turned in on the lathe.

The compote stems varied considerably. Generally it is a tapered cone about three inches tall and about one half of an inch wide at the bottom and about an inch wide at the top. Most were spiral fluted, similar to Jensen's, but some had double twists, some had vertical flutes, and many were plain with no fluting at all. There is a small "spacer" bowl between the bowl and the stem. It is a shallow cup with scallops filed out and is the structure that holds the grape vines and clusters. The grape clusters offered scope for deMatteo to vary virtually every piece. There are any number of clusters and their size varies widely. Occasionally, he made this piece with lily bud castings in place of grapes and naturally he made some naked examples with no grapes at all. The number 69 compote was a staple at deMatteo's shop and he made them for decades, often a dozen or more at one time. It is a good example of deMatteo taking inspiration from an existing and popular Jensen design for sale by Lunning in America. (Silversmith Chip deMatteo)

Three variations of compote design number 69 by William G. deMatteo. Photograph *Courtesy of Chip deMatteo*.

William G. deMatteo's record cards for Compotes #69- Grape spiral, #70- plain spiral, #71- Lily wreath spiral. *Courtesy of Chip deMatteo*

Small round and lidded sugar bowl by William G. deMatteo, 3" diameter x 4" high. This was a standard sugar bowl design that William G. deMatteo made before he started working with Frederick Lunning for the New York store. *Courtesy of Chip deMatteo*

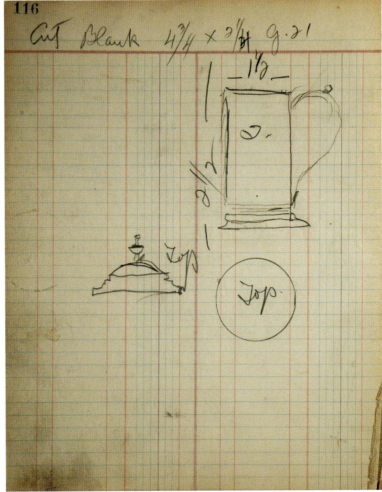

William G. deMatteo's design records book, page 116. "Cut Blank 4 ¾ x 2 ¼ g21, Top." *Courtesy of Chip deMatteo*

Marks for Georg Jensen, Inc. U.S.A. as used by William G. deMatteo, c. 1945-1948. *Courtesy of Chip deMatteo*

This version of his sugar bowl was made by William G. deMatteo to suit Frederik Lunning's preference for detailed ornament. It has a raised foot and bud decoration in the Danish style. 4" diameter x 5" high. *Courtesy of Chip deMatteo*

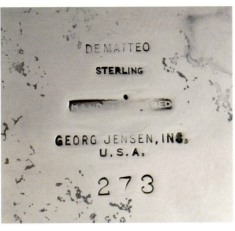

Marks for Georg Jensen, Inc. U.S.A. as used by William G. deMatteo, c. 1945-1948. *Courtesy of Chip deMatteo*

New York Store Catalogs 1944 to 1951

A 1944 Catalog

The 1944 catalog for the Georg Jensen Inc. shop in New York ("copyright, 1943, Georg Jensen Inc. New York, Printed in U.S.A.") is prefaced by this message, signed by Frederik Lunning:

For each of us, beauty has its own meaning, its individual manifestation. For this reason, we will differ in our definitions, and each of us will choose to possess those things which most satisfy our own longings.

But we all will agree that beauty, whatever form it may take, will possess perfection as that attribute which will distinguish it from all lesser objects. Thus, though you will see many forms of art exhibited at Georg Jensen Inc., you will discover that in every form a high standard of perfection is the first determinant of our merchandising policy.

The second principle which guides our policy is that of utility. We believe that objects of beauty should be not only admired, but used. As you inspect our merchandise you will see that all of it is designed to bring additional grace and ease to your daily living.

Directed in our choice by the ideals of beauty and usefulness, it is not strange that the foremost museums of the world have placed many of our pieces in their permanent collections.

To be so honored is naturally very gratifying, but it is for you, who can enjoy such beauty in you own homes, that our collection has been created. We hope that you may find this catalog a pleasant impression of our merchandise and a helpful guide in your choice of gifts.

Sincerely yours,

[signature] Frederik Lunning, President

This 1944 Georg Jensen Inc. catalog does not mention the origins or makers of the luxury goods shown, but that individual pieces are "Beautiful examples of Georg Jensen's designs." The catalog includes items of sterling silver, fine table and bed linens, crystal, china, figurines, lamps, gold jewelry, silver jewelry, clocks and watches, leather desk sets, handbags, accessories including Georg Jensen perfume "Flora Danica," furniture, metals (pewter-ware, enamel ware small ashtrays, stainless steel cookware), wooden salad bowls, and stationery.

The 1944 Georg Jensen Inc. catalog's silver section includes American style bowls in several sizes, with the following descriptions:

All the delight of colonial silver is captured again in our reproductions of the famous Paul Revere bowl.

A reproduction of the original "Sons of Liberty" bowl of 1768... The "Sons of Liberty" bowl was made for the Massachusetts House of Representatives in 1758 by Paul Revere, symbolizing Massachusetts' defiance of the King's repressive measures against self-government in the Colonies.

Lunning must have felt required to identify the American styles to his American audience, as though they were new to the Jensen line. The descriptions of silver items continue:

Companion ladles indispensable for gracious serving in our exquisite handmade Lexington pattern, designed for serving berries, compotes and dressings.

The catalog also shows:

Further Paul Revere reproductions: The frontier life of our forefathers influenced the simplicity of designs in the Colonial period. Today, these designs are still in good taste because of that simplicity.

15. All the delight of colonial silver is captured again in our reproductions of the famous Paul Revere bowl. Made in many sizes for a variety of uses: from punch and trophies to nuts and candy. (A) A reproduction of the original "Sons of Liberty" bowl of 1768, $225.00. The "Sons of Liberty" bowl was made for the Massachusetts House of Representatives in 1768 by Paul Revere, symbolizing Massachusetts' defiance of the King's repressive measures against self-government in the Colonies. (B) 13" in diameter, $110.00; (C) 11" in diameter, $82.50; (D) 10", $55.00; (E) 9", $46.50; (F) 8", $35.00; (G) 7", $27.50; (H) 6", $24.00; (I) 5", $19.25; (J) 4", $13.50; (K) 3¾", $7.90.

PAGE 6

Companion ladles indispensible for gracious serving in our exquisite handmade Lexington pattern, designed for serving berries, compotes and dressings. (L) $12.00; (M) $10.75; (N) $8.25; (O) $6.50; (P) $5.95; (Q) $5.00.

Page 6 of the Georg Jensen, Inc. New York 1944 catalog.

16. This graceful 3-piece coffee set is a PAUL REVERE reproduction with gadroon border. Complete, $137.00. Coffee pot, 1¼ pints capacity. This American made coffee service of simple and graceful lines brings forth the beauty inherent in silver when worked by master craftsmen.

17. Further Paul Revere reproductions: The frontier life of our forefathers influenced the simplicity of designs in the Colonial period. Today, these designs are still in good taste because of that simplicity. Muffinier, $27.50; Candlestick, $35.00; Salt and pepper shakers, each $8.25; Tea sieve with stand, $28.00; Candlesnuffer, $7.00.

18. The famous Paul Revere cider jug, faithfully copied by American Silversmiths: Ideal for water or milk pitchers, 4 sizes. (A) 5 pints, $66.00; (B) 3½ pints, $55.00; (C) 1⅞ pints, $44.00; (D) 1 pint, $37.00.

"All our silver is sterling, heavy weight"

PAGE 7

Page 7 of the Georg Jensen, Inc. New York 1944 catalog.

Also, it includes:

The famous Paul Revere cider jug [in four sizes], faithfully copied by American Silversmiths: Ideal for water or milk pitchers.

It is quite likely that the reproduction American style silver hollowware described in the Georg Jensen Inc. 1944 catalog was made by William G. deMatteo, silversmith of New Jersey.

19. For the woman with a real flair for gracious serving, we suggest this entirely simple and charming tea service. It was made to be a companion of ladies at tea before an open fire. The simple dignity of this 7-piece tea service may well mark it as your most important gift. Rosewood handles complete its air of elegance. $809.50. Pie crust wooden tray, $6.50.

20. Suggested gift for those who indulge in pampered service. Silver sugar basin and creamer, each $12.25. Tray finished in walnut or ebony, $2.50.

21. (A) Practical serving dish with hand-chased beaded base for sandwiches, salads and desserts, $40; (B) Server, handmade Lexington pattern, $14.25. (C) Ladle. Lexington pattern, $6.50; (D) Matching sauce bowl, $15.

22. Coffee for two before the fire will be more charming if served in this Reproduction of Early American coffee set with light wood handles. (1¼ pint coffee pot). Three-piece set, $229.25. Sugar scissors, $10.00. Matching pie crust tray, $5.50.

PAGE 8

Page 8 of the Georg Jensen, Inc. New York 1944 catalog.

Gifts for the host and hostess: useful cocktail, hors d'oeuvre and smoking accessories.

23. Juice Strainer, $10.00. Hinged measuring spoon, $12.00; with case, $13.00.

24. Bar set: (A) Corkscrew, $22.50; (B) Bottle opener, $8.40; (C) Jigger, $14.25; (D) Ice pick, $7.35; (E) Corkscrew, $14.50.

25. You don't want your furniture marked, so use these wood and silver coasters. You do want your liquor marked, so use these silver decanter labels. Coasters, $2.25 each. Labels: Whiskey, $3.50; Rum, $2.50; Port, $3.00; Gin, $2.25. Also available in Rye, $2.50; Scotch, $3.50; Bourbon, $4.50; Sherry, $3.50; Claret, $4.50.

26A. For those who smoke: (A) Modern design cigarette box, $45.00; (B) Ashtray, $9.25; (C) Ashtray, $4.50; (D) Matchbox, $4.35; (E) Matchbox, $2.00.

26B. In the frontier pattern: (A) Bottle opener, $3.75; (B) Sugar spoon, $4.00; (C) Cheese server, $3.50; (D) Jelly server, $4.00; (E) Olive or pickle fork, $2.75.

27. Glass bowl with silver base, $5.25. 4-piece hors d'oeuvre set in our exclusive handmade design. Sauce ladle, $6.60; Jelly spoon, $7.70; Spreader, $7.50; fork, $5.50.

28. Hors d'oeuvre service in the Onslow pattern: (top) Spreader with steel blade, $10.00; Crystal bowl, $4.00; Mixing spoon, $11.50; Bottle opener, $9.00.

29. Divided glass bowl with cherry or ebony tray, $6.00. The silver accessories are handmade. Ladle, $6.00; Fork, $5.00; Salt dish with enamel lining in blue or green, $15.00; plain, $10.00; Salt spoon with enamel, $3.00; plain, $2.50; Pepper shaker with enamel top, $17.00; plain, $15.00.

"All our silver is sterling, heavy weight"

PAGE 9

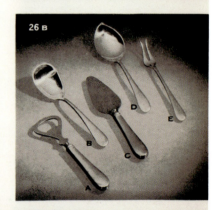

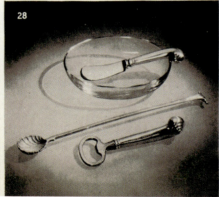

Page 9 of the Georg Jensen, Inc. New York 1944 catalog.

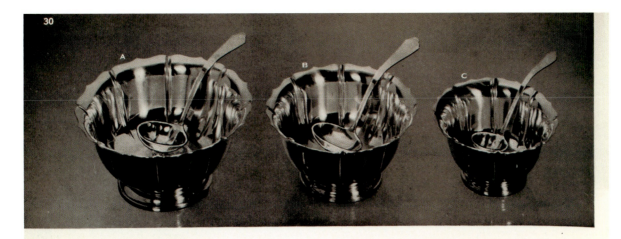

30. These fluted bowls, American reproductions of the famous "Dublin Bowl," are further enhanced by the matching ladles. Grand for the serving of vegetables, fruit and compotes. They are decorative as a centerpiece with flowers. (A) 7″ diameter, $45.00; fluted ladle, $7.75; (B) 6″ diameter, $38.00; Ladle, $6.00; (C) 5″ diameter, $24.00; Fluted Ladle, $4.75.

31. Pipkins . . . perfect for the serving of sauces, dressings, and gravies. Delightful gifts for the bride who likes to entertain. (A) $25.00; (B) $10.00.

32. The charm of these pieces is apparent in their clear and unadorned lines. Luxurious table service in restrained simplicity. Place plate, $40.00. Salt and pepper shakers, reproduction of the George Washington sand shaker, $15.00 the pair.

33. Compliment your table with this enticing vegetable dish, $38.00; Serving set in our Frontier pattern, $15.60.

"All our silver is sterling, heavy weight"

34. Now, as never before, your serving platter is the all important piece. These will be useful in many ways. The flat platter, $150.00; Well and Tree platter, $220.00. Carving sets in Frontier, Winthrop and Old Hampshire patterns with stainless steel blades, each, $24.00.

PAGE 10

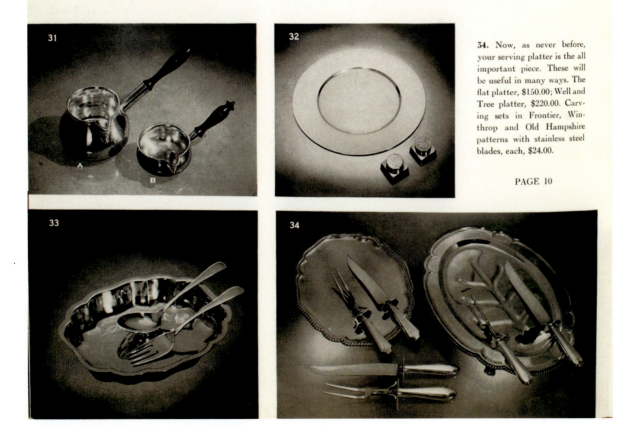

Page 10 of the Georg Jensen, Inc. New York 1944 catalog.

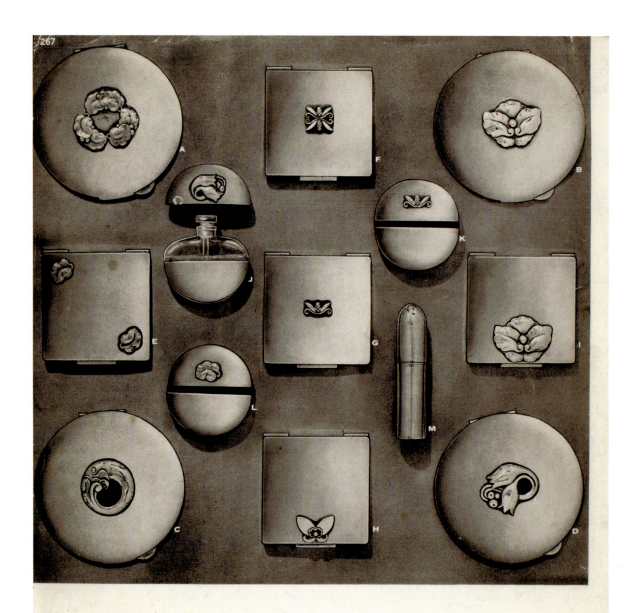

A touch of elegance for her. Sterling silver compacts and perfume flasks with Jensen motifs.

267. Flapjack compacts. Luxuriously large but pleasingly thin with tapering edges. 3½" in diameter. $50 each. (A) Leaf Wreath; (B) Heartsease; (C) Baby Dolphin; (D) Twin Tulip.

Square compacts, 2½" square, $25 each. (E) Twin Leaves; (F) Twin Acorns; (G) Acorn; (H) Cactus; (I) Heartsease. Purse perfume "portables" with glass flasks encased in silver. 2" in diameter. $11 each. (J) Twin Tulip; (K) Acorn; (L) Leaf; (M) Unique cylindrical perfume flask in sterling. Patented. Wasteproof—releases only one drop at a time. 3" high, ⅝" in diameter. $15.

(opposite page) Gold and sterling gifts for men. Suggestions to fill your masculine gift needs from one year's end to another.

280. (A) Sterling identification bracelet. Heavy, slim, and narrow, $16.50.

(B) Sterling identification bracelet. Extra heavy yet streamlined. $19.25.

(C) Sterling identification bracelet. Heavy with wide plaque, $16.50.

(D) "Rollalite" cigarette lighter, 14k gold cased. $137.50.

(E) St. Christopher medal in 10k gold. Image in relief. On reverse side impression of steamship, auto, airplane, and train in relief. $15.

PAGE 40

Page 40 of the Georg Jensen, Inc. New York 1944 catalog.

Seven full pages of silver jewelry shown in the 1944 Georg Jensen Inc. catalog are likely items made by Americn silversmith Alphonse LaPaglia of New Jersey, although their maker is not identified in the catalog. Many of the hollowware and jewelry styles shown resemble Georg Jensen of Copenhagen styles, while some match pieces made and marked before or after this time period by William G. deMatteo and Alphonse La Paglia.

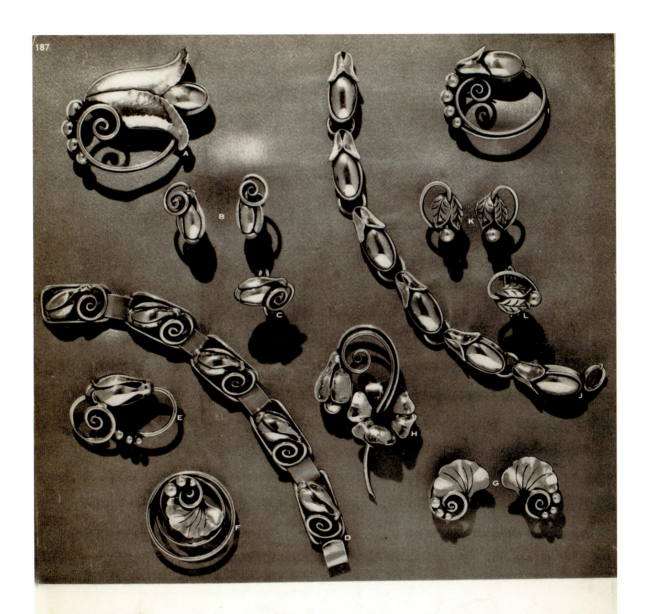

Silver Jewelry

Silver jewelry in dramatic patterns and effective silhouettes. All pieces are sterling and handmade.

187. (A) Tulip Swirl brooch, subtly hammered, set with silver ball, $20.

A delightful group in Snowdrop design: (B) Earrings, pair, $14; (C) Ring, $14; (D) Bracelet, $45; (E) Brooch, $14.

(F) "Leaf in Whirlpool": an eye-catching ornament. Brooch, $12; (G) Earrings to match, $14 a pair.

(H) Lapel Spray in Snowdrop design, $15; (I) Flora Wreath with silver ball, $14.

A matched set in Bud design possessing distinction through its very simplicity: (J) Bracelet, effectively set with silver balls, $60; (K) Earrings, $12 a pair; (L) Ring, $12.

PAGE 34

Page 34 of the Georg Jensen, Inc. New York 1944 catalog.

203. Narcissus, a design that has captured in silver the very freshness of spring flowers.

(A) Choker, ribbon-like in its smoothly lying contour, $55;

(B) Bracelet, $25.

(C) Brooch, $14; (D) Earrings, $12 a pair.

(E) Brooch, with dainty treatment of wheat stalks sway-ing with the breeze, $19; (F) Bracelet, $25; (G) Earrings, $10 a pair.

Medallion design: an attractive combination of quaintly stylized flowers against a modern silver background.

(H) Brooch, effective as two clips, or when worn with straight sides together as a bar pin, $10 each.

(I) Bracelet with tiny bright flowers appliquéd on an ox-idized background, $40.

"All our silver jewelry is sterling, heavy weight and handmade"

Page 35 of the Georg Jensen, Inc. New York 1944 catalog.

212. (A) Posy pin lapel vase actually holds water in a sponge to keep flowers fresh. $5.50.

(B) The satin-like finish of this bracelet is accentuated by the Fan Leaf design. $55.

(C) Clip brooches of Cactus design. Effective worn in a pair. $9 each.

(D) "Bluebell Swirl", a drama in shadows and silver. $18.

(E) Lapel brooch in Bluebell design, $15.

(F) Bluebells for the ear lobes, $12.50 a pair.

(G) Flowering Cactus, a novel brooch of modern design, $18.
(H) Earrings to match, $11 the pair.

(I) An amusing brooch. You may choose from a variety of stones to light the open eye of this peek-a-boo kitten, $13.50

(J) A beguiling lapel locket in Acorn design, equally effective worn against black or the bright, warm colors of the season, $23.
(K) Matching earrings, $15 a pair.

(L) Earrings. Fragile shells set within silver halos. Pair, $7.50.

(M) A brooch of silver bubbles to accent your tailored clothes, $11.
(N) Ring to match, $12.50.

PAGE 36

Page 36 of the Georg Jensen, Inc. New York 1944 catalog.

230. Companion pieces, well-named "Forget-me-not."
(A) Choker, $65; (B) Bracelet, $30.

Two Brooches: (C) "Leaf and Fruit", $16; (D) Piquant Pansy, $9.

(E) A luxurious bracelet of autumn leaves and berries, $30; (F) Earrings to match, $10.

(G) A delicate and lovely gift is this bracelet of Danish Rose design, $35; (H) Matching earrings, $13.

(I) Brooch in Heartsease design, $7.50.

(J) The lapel locket, decorated with a trio of tulips, holds two pictures, $25.

(K) Twin tulips for the ears, $16 a pair.

You will be long remembered for your thoughtfulness if you give her this lovely, useful set of two hatpins and a pair of earrings.
(L) In Calla Lily design, $25 complete. (M) The same set in Buttercup design, $20.

PAGE 37

Page 37 of the Georg Jensen, Inc. New York 1944 catalog

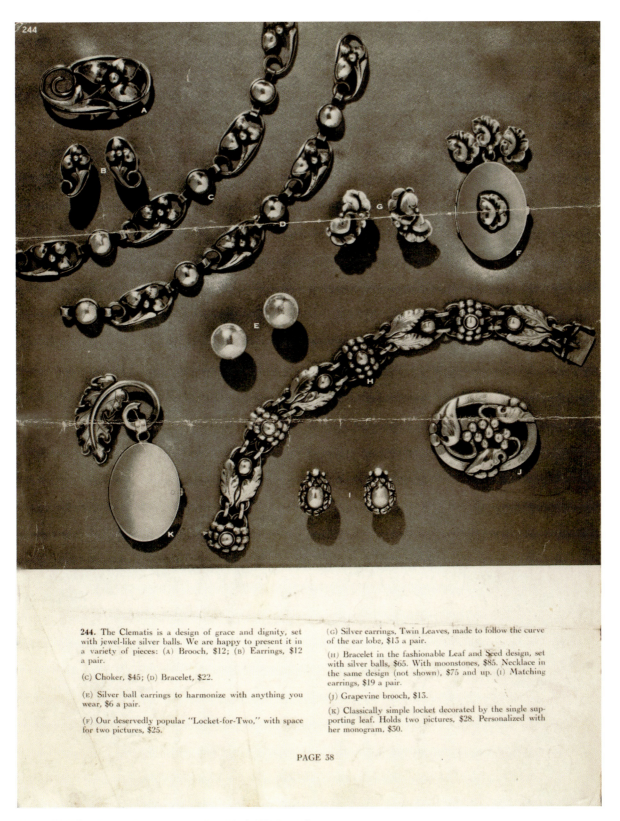

244. The Clematis is a design of grace and dignity, set with jewel-like silver balls. We are happy to present it in a variety of pieces: (A) Brooch, $12; (B) Earrings, $12 a pair.

(C) Choker, $45; (D) Bracelet, $22.

(E) Silver ball earrings to harmonize with anything you wear, $6 a pair.

(F) Our deservedly popular "Locket-for-Two," with space for two pictures, $25.

(G) Silver earrings, Twin Leaves, made to follow the curve of the ear lobe, $13 a pair.

(H) Bracelet in the fashionable Leaf and Seed design, set with silver balls, $65. With moonstones, $85. Necklace in the same design (not shown), $75 and up. (I) Matching earrings, $19 a pair.

(J) Grapevine brooch, $13.

(K) Classically simple locket decorated by the single supporting leaf. Holds two pictures, $28. Personalized with her monogram, $30.

PAGE 38

Page 38 of the Georg Jensen, Inc. New York 1944 catalog.

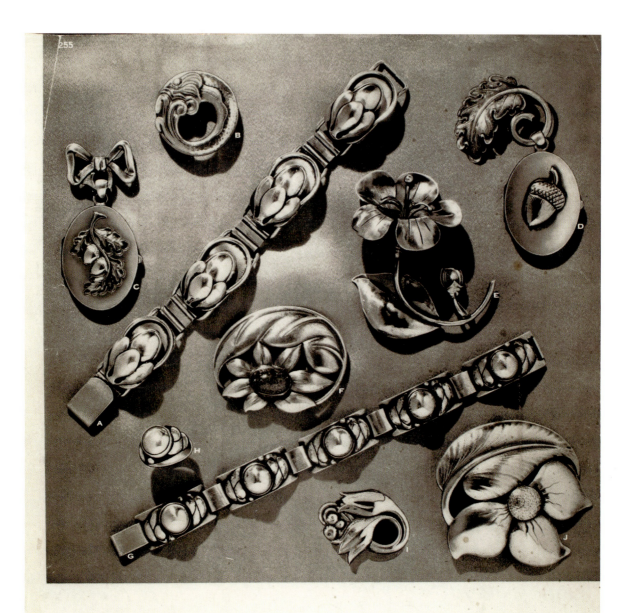

255. (A) Bracelet of massive Water Lily design, set with luminous silver balls, $60.

(B) Baby Dolphin brooch, $8.

Two lockets that will win a high place in your personal collection. Both are handmade in repoussé style and have space for two pictures. (C) Oak Cluster, with Bowknot pin, $40. (D) Acorn Fantasy, $38.

(E) Morning Glory lapel pin very realistically executed in silver, $40.

(F) This brooch shows novel treatment of the Daisy motif with moonstone center, $50.

(G) Bracelet in the Leaf design set with large silver balls. $40.

(H) Ring, also in the Leaf, with pearl-like silver ball, $12.

(I) The perfect "little" brooch in the Twin Tulip design. Or use a pair as clips. Each, $8.

(J) Beautiful handmade repoussé Dahlia brooch $35.

PAGE 39

Page 39 of the Georg Jensen, Inc. New York 1944 catalog.

Frederik Lunning continued to run his shop and business after the war ended in Europe in 1945, but the goods he had sold before the war were not quickly replaced by the Georg Jensen workshop in Copenhagen. Lunning continued to carry America-made goods in New York for the next few years. The few silver items from the Copenhagen workshop that did reach the New York store between 1945 and 1951 were clearly marked in Copenhagen, "Georg Jensen & Wendell A/S, Denmark."

In 1947 Frederik Lunning's son, Just Lunning (1910-1965), became mature and worked with his father to promote and sell goods in the Georg Jensen Inc. New York shop. Just Lunning was instrumental in setting up branches of the New York store in a few of the surrounding suburban communities of Scarsdale and Manhasset, New York, and in Millburn, New Jersey.

A 1947 Catalog

When Georg Jensen silver from Copenhagen gradually began to become available in New York again after the war, Lunning continued to market the range of other luxury goods as well. In a Georg Jensen Inc. catalog for 1947, only the first two of 71 pages contain silver items from the Copenhagen Georg Jensen workshops. Designs by Georg Jensen, Johan Rohde, Sigvard Bernadotte, and others appear, labeled "Imported Silver." In the jewelry section of the catalog, text refers to "old favorites...and the introduction of the work of several talented young newcomers whose craftsmanship so obviously and definitely expresses the feeling in jewelry we are constantly seeking...some of the new names are: Bjarne Meyer, Maria Regnier, Anna Halasi, A. LaPaglia, M. Cusick and others. (Drucker, *Georg Jensen: A Tradition of Splendid Silver*, page 52)

A 1948 Catalog

Cover of the Georg Jensen, Inc. New York, 1948 catalog. *Courtesy of Romance with Silver Collection*

Danish Rose design link bracelet made and marked "GJ", by Georg Jensen, Copenhagen, with links matching the bracelet and earrings appearing on page 37 of the 1944 catalog of items for sale by Georg Jensen Inc. U.S.A.

Bar pin, as shown on page 36 in the 1944 catalog and in the 1951 cagalog for the New York store, 1.75" long. Made by Georg Jensen, Denmark. *Courtesy of Dr. Morton & Maidie Kaplon of Summit, New Jersey.*

The 1948 catalog of items from the Georg Jensen Inc. store in New York is more revealing. On page two of the catalog, under a heading titled "Silver Treasures," the following explanation is offered:

> George Jensen Inc. presents the matchless elegance of sterling, created by LaPaglia and deMatteo, craftsmen, who have a knowledge of the metal and a fine feeling for proportion and dignity. Their pieces are characteristic of the beautiful silver to be found in this shop, the name of which has always been a synonym for perfection in sterling.

The next fifteen items (numbers 21 through 37, including several pieces in some of the sets) are individually identified as having been made "by DeMatteo" or "by La Paglia." This catalog is unique in mentioning these two American silversmiths by name.

Page 2 of the Georg Jensen, Inc. New York, 1948 catalog. *Courtesy of Romance with Silver Collection*

Page 3 of the Georg Jensen, Inc. New York, 1948 catalog. *Courtesy of Romance with Silver Collection*

The next page of the 1948 catalog for the Georg Jensen Inc. store in New York contains a group titled, "Fine American Sterling." The pieces shown in photographs and identified in words are not attributed to a silversmith, but demonstrate particularly American styles. The items include (42 C) a "Water pitcher, copy of the famous Paul Revere cider jug," and (42 E) a "Cream and suger set, replica in miniature of Paul Revere bowl and pitcher." Other examples are equally derivative of American designs rather than the Danish modern designs of Georg Jensen in Copenhagen.

Page 4 of the Georg Jensen, Inc. New York, 1948 catalog. *Courtesy of Romance with Silver Collection*

Page 5 of the Georg Jensen, Inc. New York, 1948 catalog. *Courtesy of Romance with Silver Collection*

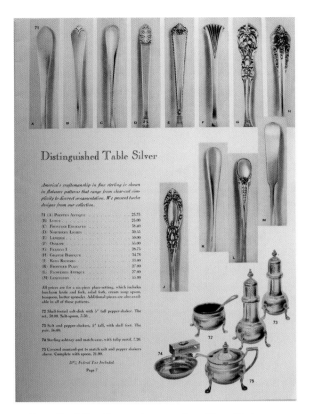

Page 7 of the Georg Jensen, Inc. New York 1948 catalog. *Courtesy of Romance with Silver Collection*

Continuing through the 1948 catalog, the section titled "Distinguished Table Silver" begins with the explanation:

America's craftsmanship in fine sterling is shown in flatware patterns that range from clear-cut simplicity to discreet ornamentation. We present twelve designs from our collection.

The 1948 catalog's section titled "Silver Jewelry" runs for three pages and displays styles consistent with the Danish modern designs of Georg Jensen as interpreted by American silversmith Alphonse La Paglia.

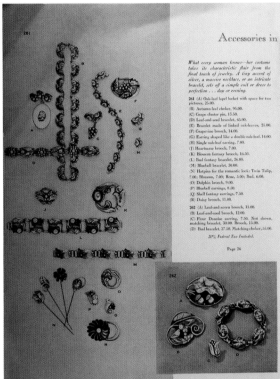

Page 26 of the Georg Jensen, Inc. New York, 1948 catalog. *Courtesy of Romance with Silver Collection*

Page 25 of the Georg Jensen, Inc. New York, 1948 catalog. *Courtesy of Romance with Silver Collection*

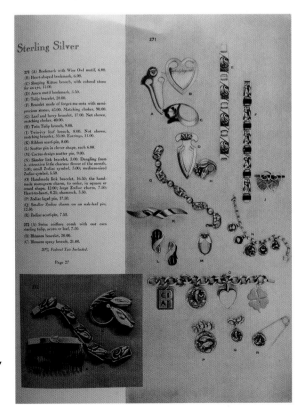

Page 27 of the Georg Jensen, Inc. New York, 1948 catalog. *Courtesy of Romance with Silver Collection*

Another 1948 Catalog

The Georg Jensen Inc. shop at 667 Fifth Avenue put out another catalog in 1948, marked on the title page "1948 Georg Jensen Inc. presents..." It may have preceded or followed in time the catalog mentioned above. In this other catalog we find a section titled "American Silver" shown on four catalog pages (2 through 5), without mention of any silversmiths and the descriptions are abbreviated. The pictured items are American styles, rather than Danish styles.

Page 2 of a Georg Jensen Inc. New York, 1948 catalog. *Courtesy of Romance with Silver Collection*

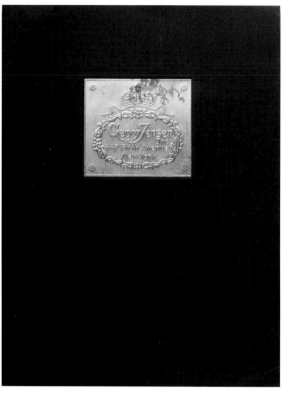

Cover of a Georg Jensen Inc. New York, 1948 catalog. *Courtesy of Romance with Silver Collection*

Page 3 of a Georg Jensen Inc. New York, 1948 catalog. *Courtesy of Romance with Silver Collection*

Page 1 of a Georg Jensen Inc. New York, 1948 catalog. *Courtesy of Romance with Silver Collection*

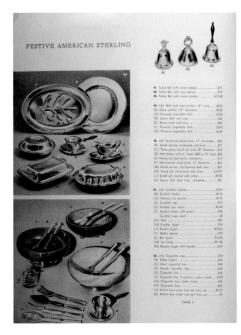

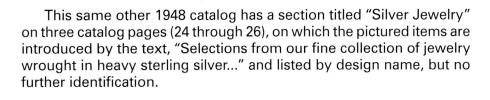

This same other 1948 catalog has a section titled "Silver Jewelry" on three catalog pages (24 through 26), on which the pictured items are introduced by the text, "Selections from our fine collection of jewelry wrought in heavy sterling silver..." and listed by design name, but no further identification.

Page 4 of a Georg Jensen Inc. New York, 1948 catalog. *Courtesy of Romance with Silver Collection*

Page 24 of a Georg Jensen Inc. New York, 1948 catalog. *Courtesy of Romance with Silver Collectionv*

Page 26 of a Georg Jensen Inc. New York, 1948 catalog. *Courtesy of Romance with Silver Collection*

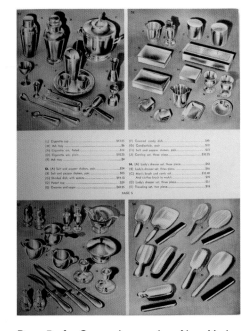

Page 5 of a Georg Jensen Inc. New York, 1948 catalog. *Courtesy of Romance with Silver Collection*

Page 25 of a Georg Jensen Inc. New York, 1948 catalog. *Courtesy of Romance with Silver Collection*

A 1951 Catalog

Another catalog of luxury goods for sale by the New York store Georg Jensen Inc. was issued in 1951. The front three pages (2, 3, and 4) display photographs and descriptions of items entitled "Georg Jensen Silver," and these are classic Danish items made by the George Jensen workshops in Copenhagen.

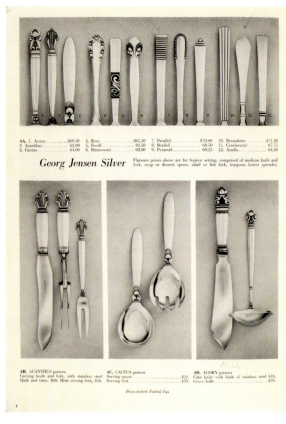

Page 1 of the Georg Jensen Inc. New York, 1951 catalog. *Courtesy of Romance with Silver Collection*

Page 4 of the Georg Jensen Inc. New York, 1951 catalog. *Courtesy of Romance with Silver Collection*

Page 2 of the Georg Jensen Inc. New York, 1951 catalog. *Courtesy of Romance with Silver Collection*

Page 3 of the Georg Jensen Inc. New York, 1951 catalog. *Courtesy of Romance with Silver Collection*

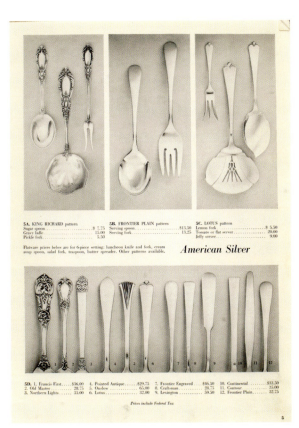

Page 5 of the Georg Jensen Inc. New York, 1951 catalog. *Courtesy of Romance with Silver Collection*

The next three pages (5, 6, and 7) are entitled "American Silver," and they display photographs and brief descriptions of silver flatware and hollowware in American styles, not in Danish styles.

Page 6 of the Georg Jensen Inc. New York, 1951 catalog. *Courtesy of Romance with Silver Collection*

Page 7 of the Georg Jensen Inc. New York, 1951 catalog. *Courtesy of Romance with Silver Collection*

The catalog continues with two pages (8 and 9) of crystal tableware, some identified as "from Holland, a lovely Leerdam crystal candy dish..." and as "Swedish Orrefors crystal..." Page 10 offers "linen by Margghab" and pages 11 through 13 display china, metal, and wooden table ware.

Further back in the 1951 Georg Jensen Inc. catalog are silver jewelry items. Pages 14 through 16 display items entitled "Georg Jensen Silver" and these are products from the Copenhagen workshops. Pages 16 and 17 display items entitled "American Silver," and they are similar in style to those shown in the 1944 and 1948 catalogs of George Jensen Inc. of New York.

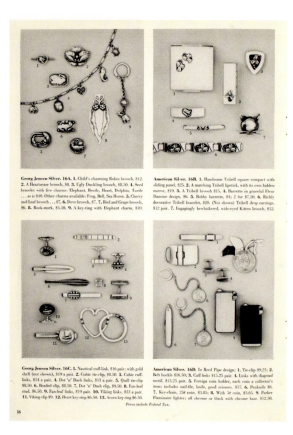

Page 17 of the Georg Jensen Inc. New York, 1951 catalog. *Courtesy of Romance with Silver Collection*

Page 16 of the Georg Jensen Inc. New York, 1951 catalog. *Courtesy of Romance with Silver Collection*

The remaining seven pages (18 to 24) of the 1951 catalog display non-silver jewelry, clocks, watches, stationery, furniture, leather desk sets, "Royal Copenhagen Porcelain" figurines, leather handbags, accessories, children's clothing, and "a spirited rocking horse." Clearly, this catalog includes American, Danish, and other imported items, which indicates that trade with Europe was being restored by this time for items that were displayed in the American shops of Georg Jensen Inc.

Pomegranate candlesticks No. 324 by Georg Jensen silversmith of Copenhagen, a gift from the Georg Jensen A/S company to Frederik Lunning on the occasion of his 70th birthday, "21-12-1951."

Jewelry and Hollowware

When shipments of silver goods from the Georg Jensen workshop in Copenhagen were reinstated, the production of silver by American silversmiths for the Georg Jensen Inc. store in New York was no longer essential. An agreement between Frederik Lunning and the Georg Jensen company directors in Copenhagen was worked out in 1951, formally ending the production and sale of American-made silver marked "Georg Jensen Inc, U.S.A." Therefore, items of sterling silver found today that bear the marks of silversmiths with the shop mark of "Georg Jensen Inc. U.S.A." can safely be dated to the period about 1940 to 1951.

Floral pin made and marked by Alphonse La Paglia for Georg Jensen, Inc. U.S.A. *Courtesy of Carmen Armstrong, Adornments Unlimited*

Necklace and bracelet set, silver rope chain by Alphonse La Paglia for Georg Jensen. Inc. U.S.A. 8" bracelet, 16" necklace. *Courtesy of Third Floor Antiques*.

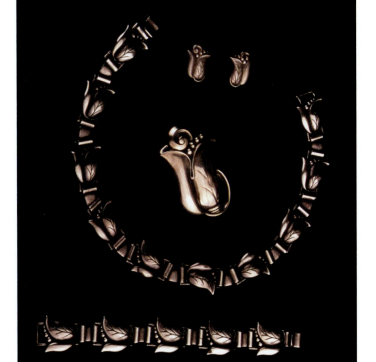

Fleur Danoise design link necklace, bracelet, earrings, and brooch/pendant made and marked by Alphonse La Paglia for Georg Jensen Inc. U.S.A. This jewelry pattern appears in the 1948 catalog of Georg Jensen Inc. U.S.A.

Bud design link necklace and bracelet, and earrings made and marked by Alphonse La Paglia for Georg Jensen Inc. U.S.A. This jewelry pattern appears in the 1948 catalog of Georg Jensen Inc. U.S.A.

Fluted bowl #248 by William G. deMatteo for Georg Jensen, Inc. 7 ½" diameter. *Courtesy of Chip deMatteo*

William G. deMatteo's design records book, page 1, c. 1948, for designs #200 to #231. The entry after #210, for #17 A, reads "Bowl – G.J. –". *Courtesy of Chip deMatteo*

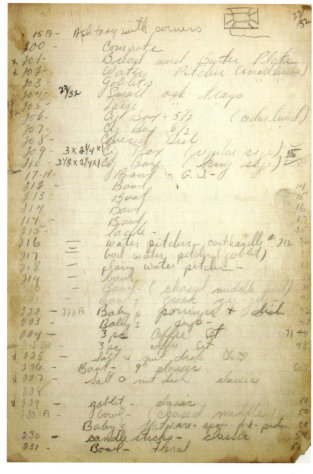

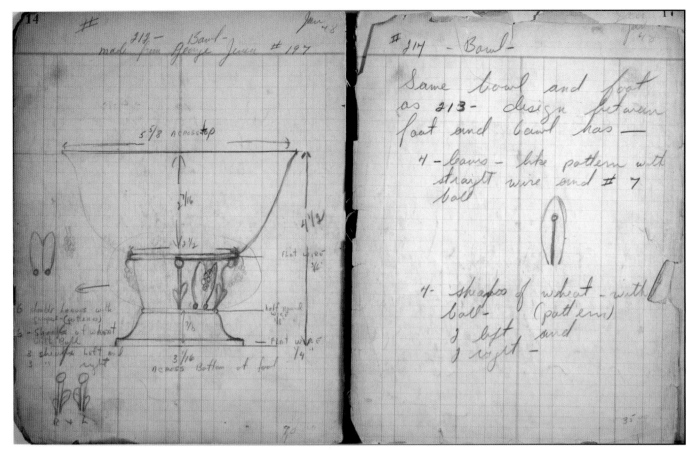

William G. deMatteo's design records book, pages 14 and 15. Left page showing design "#212- Bowl made for Georg Jensen #197," dated Jan. [19]48. Right page describes design #214 Bowl, as "Same bowl and foot as 213- design fret w--- font and bowl has—4- leaves – like pattern with straight wire and #7 ball   4-sheafs of wheat – with ball- (pattern) 2 left and 2 right –.". *Courtesy of Chip deMatteo*

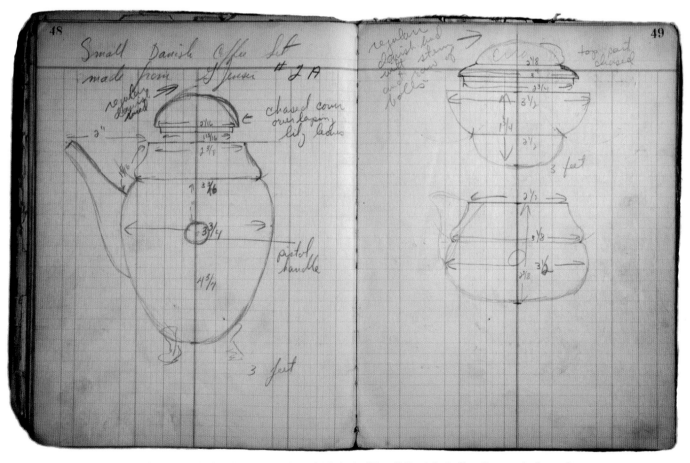

William G. deMatteo's design records book, pages 48 and 49. Left, "Small Danish Coffee Set made from G Jensen #2A, regular Danish bud, chased cover overlapping lily leaves, pistol handle, 3 feet. Right, "regular Danish bud with stem and row of balls, top part chased, 3 feet." *Courtesy of Chip deMatteo*

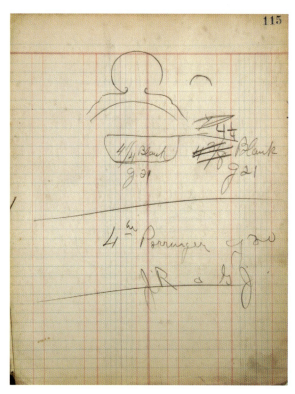

Scalloped vegetable dish #132 by Alphonse La Paglia for Georg Jensen, Inc. U.S.A. 1.75 tall, 9 x 8.5. *Courtesy of Dr. Morton & Maidie Kaplon of Summit, New Jersey.*

William G. deMatteo's design records book, page 115. "4- Porringer, J R & G J." *Courtesy of Chip deMatteo*

Footed vegetable #160, 3 ½" x 9 ¼" x 3 ¾" high. Marked under the rim Georg Jensen Inc. U.S.A. (no other silversmith's mark). *Courtesy of Romance with Silver Collection*

Jensen-style pitcher with ebony handle made by William G. deMatteo, 9" high. *Courtesy of Chip deMatteo*

Jensen-style pitcher made by William G. deMatteo, 9" high. *Courtesy of Chip deMatteo*

Six cordials. 2 on right marked Georg Jensen U.S.A. LP; middle three marked International Sterling L. Paglia Designed; left is smaller with no mark and slight pattern variation. *Courtesy of Dr. Morton & Maidie Kaplon of Summit, New Jersey*

Designs by Alphonse La Paglia

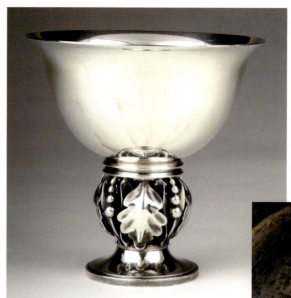

Pedestal bowl #151 with leaf and bead pattern base by Alphonse La Paglia for Georg Jensen, Inc. U.S.A., 5.25" x 5". *Courtesy of Dr. Morton & Maidie Kaplon of Summit, New Jersey.*

Footed bowl #114 by Alphonse La Paglia for Georg Jensen Inc. U.S.A. 5 ¼" x 3 ¾" high. *Courtesy of Romance with Silver Collection*

Jensen-style cup with a cast foot, by William G. deMatteo, 5" high. *Courtesy of Chip deMatteo*

Salt dish #117 by Alphonse La Paglia for Georg Jensen Inc. U.S.A., 2 ½″ x 3 ¼″ x 1 ½″ high. *Courtesy of Romance with Silver Collection*

Two footed candy dishes #105 by Alphonse La Paglia for Georg Jensen. Inc. U.S.A., 5″ x 3 ¾″ x 1.5″ high. *Courtesy of Romance with Silver Collection*

Celery dish #108 by Alphonse La Paglia for Georg Jensen Inc. U.S.A., 13 ¼″ x 6 ½″ x 2 ¼″ high. *Courtesy of Romance with Silver Collection*

Comparison of a vegetable dish #112 by La Paglia and a celery dish #108 by La Paglia for Georg Jensen. Inc. U.S.A. *Courtesy of Romance with Silver Collection*

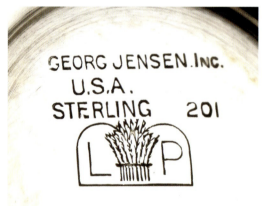

Console set of a bowl and two candlesticks by Alphonse La Paglia. Candlesticks #201 made and marked by La Paglia for Georg Jensen. Inc. U.S.A. The Bowl made and marked by La Paglia. Bowl, 10" x 3 ¾" high; candlesticks 3 ¾" d x 3" high. *Courtesy of Romance with Silver Collection*

Cream pitcher and sugar bowl #114 by Alphonse La Paglia for Georg Jensen Inc. U.S.A., creamer 4 ½", sugar 3 5/8". *Courtesy of Romance with Silver Collection*

Tall vase #116 made by Alphonse La Paglia for Georg Jensen. Inc. U.S.A. 8 ¾" x 4". *Courtesy of Romance with Silver Collection*

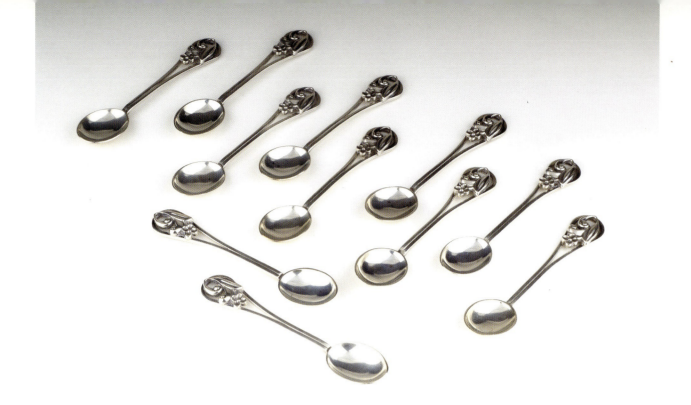

Demitasse spoons #112 made by Alphonse La Paglia for Georg Jensen. Inc. U.S.A. 4 ¼" long. *Courtesy of Romance with Silver Collection*

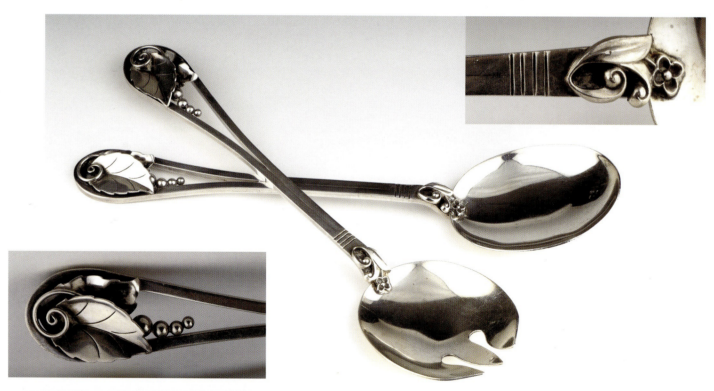

Salad servers #113 by Alphonse La Paglia for Georg Jensen Inc. U.S.A. 10 3/8" long. *Courtesy of Romance with Silver Collection*

Serving pieces #112 by Alphonse La Paglia for Georg Jensen Inc. U.S.A. spoon 5 ¼" long; spreader 7" long; fork 5 1/2" long. *Courtesy of Romance with Silver Collection*

Small ladle #131 by Alphonse La Paglia for Georg Jensen. Inc. U.S.A. 6 ¼" long. *Courtesy of Romance with Silver Collection*

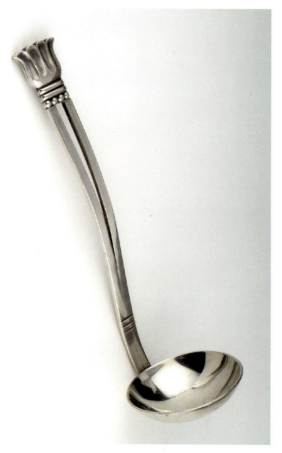

Small ladle #105 by Alphonse La Paglia for Georg Jensen. Inc. U.S.A., 5 3/8" long. *Courtesy of Romance with Silver Collection*

Small ladle #103 by Alphonse La Paglia for Georg Jensen. Inc. U.S.A., 5 ½" long. *Courtesy of Romance with Silver Collection*

Small ladle #101 by Alphonse La Paglia for Georg Jensen. Inc. U.S.A., 5 ¼" long. *Courtesy of Romance with Silver Collection*

Two cake servers with handle variations by Alphonse La Paglia for Georg Jensen. Inc. U.S.A. 10 ½" long. *Courtesy of Romance with Silver Collection*

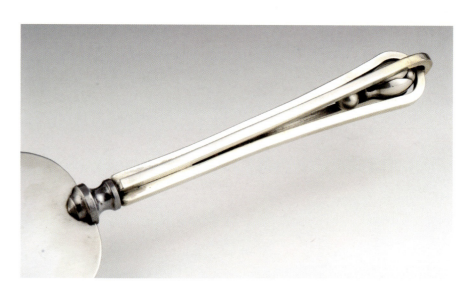

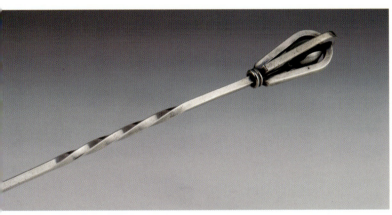

Letter opener (filigree end) by Alphonse La Paglia for Georg Jensen. Inc. U.S.A., 7 3/8" long. *Courtesy of Romance with Silver Collection*

Stirrer by Alphonse La Paglia for Georg Jensen. Inc. U.S.A., 11" long. *Courtesy of Romance with Silver Collection*

Chapter 4

Danish Modern Silver Styles Become Mainstream in America

The Frederik Lunning Prize

In order to stimulate and continue promoting modern design styles, and to encourage young artists to achieve their best potential, Frederik Lunning and Kaj Dessau, the manager of the New York Georg Jensen Inc. shop, initiated a design prize in 1950 that directly affected the history of modern design.

> Lunning had been a pioneer. With dogged stubbornness and salesmanship amounting to genius he had, in spite of everything and everybody, created a steady market in the New World for Danish silver and china. This was his main achievement. It was therefore a natural thing to advise him to consolidate this position and expand, to try to utilize the great and promising development within Nordic handicraft and decorative art, and do his best to make Georg Jensen Inc. the natural, lively, and efficient centre for the Nordic countries in America. Nobody held better cards, despite everything! He had been the first – and until 1940 – the best. But the "general store" of the years of war would have to be cleaned up – and the new objective made visible to everybody! (*The Lunning Prize*, p. 12)

The Prize was intended to showcase the best in contemporary Scandinavian design in all the decorative arts and to generate goodwill among manufacturers in Nordic countries. It also drew attention to the Georg Jensen Inc. store as the center for Nordic design in America.

The Prize was to provide for two awards a year from among entries of artists from the four Scandinavian countries: Denmark, Finland, Norway, and Sweden, but in any one year the winners could not be of the same nationality and "under no circumstances to go to a particular country more than 2 years in succession." A traveling scholarship "to support talented and original Nordic craftsmen and industrial designers – preferably young persons – for whom a carefully planned and lengthy period of study abroad stand to be of great or decisive importance for their artistic development and practical performance." (*The Lunning Prize*, p. 16)

A committee of judges was formed that carefully discussed what "*preferably young persons*" meant to the prize, what the criteria was to be, and how the judging was to be conducted. "It was never the intention that the Frederik Lunning Prize should encourage the prize-winners to emulate applied arts or design in other countries. The idea was to extend their daily work, leaving them free to have time for reflection and perhaps in completely new surroundings obtain inspiration for a fresher look at things." (*The Lunning Prize*, p. 16)

Advertisements were placed in the major national newspapers inviting cragtsmen and designers to apply for the scholarship. About 150 candidates responded, representing designs in glass, ceramics, metalwork, furniture, industrial design, jewelry, textile art, and teaching. The first awards were made on Frederik Lunning's sevetieth birthday, December 21, 1951.

The unexpected and untimely death of Frederik Lunning, on September 1, 1952, did not eclipse the prize. "The Frederik Lunning Committee acknowledges that the three childeren of Frederik Lunning who now own Georg Jensen Inc., New York, have continued their father's benevolent plans after his death, and recalls the founder of the Prize with profound veneration." (*The Lunning Prize*, p. 16) The Prize was awarded annually for twenty years.

The contest generated international exhibitions and established the concept of Scandinavain design as it promoted cooperation among Nordic designers, industries, and institutions. The New York Georg Jensen store held exhibitions of the Prize winner's work and their talents came to the attention of the parent company in Copenhagen. Several winners took a job with the Georg Jensen workshop and gained continuing recognition after receiving their Frederik Lunning Prize.

After Just Lunning, Frederik's son and heir at the New York shop, died prematurely in 1965, the Lunning family sold the business. After the last award was made in 1970 the prize funding ceased, because the new owners were not as interested in the future of the Scandinavian lines of business.

"Leaving aside the question whether the aim has been achieved, it can be said that today, Scandinavian applied art has a high reputation throughout the world. Quite a few winners of the Frederik Lunning Prize have become renowned outside their own country and nearly all of them report a great benefit from their travels." (*The Lunning Prize*, p. 16)

The Frederik Lunning Prize Winners, 1951 to 1970

1951 Hans J. Wegner, Denmark
      Tapio Wirkkala, Finland
1952 Carl-Axel Acking, Sweden
      Grete Prytz Kittelsen, Norway
1953 Tias Eckhoff, Norway
      Henning Koppel, Denmark
1954 Ingeborg Lundin, Sweden
      Jens H. Quistgaard, Denmark
1955 Ingrid Dessau, Sweden
      Kaj Franck, Finland
1956 Jørgen and Nanna Ditzel, Denmark
      Timo Sarpaneva, Finland
1957 Hermann Bongard, Norway
      Erik Höglund, Sweden
1958 Poul Kjærholm, Denmark
      Signe Persson-Melin, Sweden
1959 Arne Jon Jutrem, Norway
      Antti Nurmesniemi, Finland
1960 Vivianna Torun Bülow-Hübe, Sweden
      Vibeke Klint, Denmark
1961 Bertel Gardberg, Finland
      Erik Pløen, Norway
1962 Hertha Hillfon, Sweden
      Kristian Solmer Vedel, Denmark
1963 Karin Björquist, Sweden
      Börje Rajalin, Finland
1964 Vuokko Eskolin-Nurmesniemi, Finland

Thereafter, Georg Jensen Inc. was resold many times. But a new Georg Jensen silver company-sponsored shop rose again in New York, on Madison Avenue, when the Royal Copenhagen/Georg Jensen store opened around 1980. Today, Georg Jensen silver is produced only in Denmark, and sales continue to flourish in Georg Jensen specialty shops around the world.

Alphonse LaPaglia and International Silver, 1952

Alphonse La Paglia was an independent silversmith, and in 1952 he was contracted by the International Silver Company, of Meriden, Connecticut, to create designs for them. In 1953 La Paglia moved from Summit, New Jersey, to Connecticut, where International Silver set up a workshop for him and underwrote his designs. For International Silver, La Paglia created new designs in a sleek, modern fashion. Unfortunately, he had an accident at home, in which he fell from a roof while cleaning rain gutters and broke a leg. During his recovery, medical complications proved fatal to him. Alphonse LaPaglia died on November 19, 1953.

Alphonse La Paglia's widow, Harriette K. La Paglia, eventually sold her husband's business to the International Silver Company, which continued to produce his designs as the International Sterling Craft Associates, until at least 1954, when catalogs specifically featuring them were issued. His *La Paglia Designed* pieces gradually became modified as they were produced in large quantities, and many of the designs lost La Paglia's distinctive handmade look. Items of his designs made by International Silver bear the identifying marks of the International Silver Company.

Opposite: International Sterling *La Paglia Designed* jewelry price list for 1952

JEWELRY

NO.	ITEM	PRICE
100	Bangle	12.00
102	Bangle, square, plain	11.00
103	Bangle, large, chain twist	16.00
105	Bangle, rope, chain	15.00
107	Bangle, small, chain twist	7.00
207	Cuff Bracelet	22.00
108	Cuff Bracelet	22.00
110	Cuff Bracelet	25.00
110	Link Bracelet	55.00
125	Link Bracelet	35.00
140	Link Bracelet	35.00
141	Link Bracelet	50.00
102	Link Bracelet	35.00
143	Link Bracelet	35.00
145	Link Bracelet	30.00
146	Link Bracelet	30.00
147	Link Bracelet	30.00
148	Link Bracelet	30.00
150	Link Bracelet	30.00
212	Link Bracelet	35.00
211	Link Bracelet	20.00
213	Link Bracelet	35.00
215	Link Bracelet	25.00
217	Link Bracelet	22.00
149	Link Bracelet	30.00
230	Baby Ivy Link Bracelet	22.00
113	Link Bracelet	35.00

NO.	ITEM	PRICE
220	Link Bracelet	35.00
100	Chain Bracelet	18.00

EARRINGS

NO.	ITEM	PRICE
101	Earrings	13.00
102	Earrings	10.00
103	Earrings	15.00
105	Earrings, small	5.50
105	Earrings, medium	6.00
105	Earrings, large	7.00
113	Earrings	16.00
114	Earrings	12.00
120	Earrings	15.00
123	Earrings	15.00
124	Earrings	13.00
138	Earrings	13.00
140	Earrings	11.00
146	Earrings	10.00
147	Earrings	10.00
148	Earrings	10.00
149	Earrings	10.00
212	Earrings	12.00
112	Earrings, single leaf	12.00
145	Earrings	10.00
220	Earrings	12.00

NO.	ITEM	PRICE
BROOCHES		
101	Brooch	22.00
103	Brooch	15.00
105	Brooch	15.00
106	Brooch	22.00
107	Brooch	12.50
108	Brooch	13.00
109	Brooch	10.00
113	Brooch	10.00
114	Brooch	11.00
117	Brooch	12.00
122	Brooch	13.00
126	Brooch	18.00
128	Brooch	15.00
129	Brooch	10.00
130	Brooch	20.00
132	Brooch	15.00
133	Brooch	17.00
134	Brooch	18.00
137	Brooch	20.00
140	Brooch	12.00
153	Brooch	18.00
154	Brooch	25.00
200	Brooch	18.00
202	Brooch	18.00
205	Brooch	18.00
207	Brooch	18.00
210	Pendant, double heart, small	10.00
211	Pendant, double heart, large	11.00
212	Brooch, large	18.00

NO.	ITEM	PRICE
216	Brooch	18.00
212	Brooch, small	13.00
145	Brooch, small	12.00
145	Brooch, large	15.00
220	Brooch	15.00
218	Brooch	16.00
112	Ivy heart charm	12.00
101	Baby Cross	8.50
129	Bar Pin	10.00
NECKLACES		
100	Chain Necklace	42.00
102	Link Necklace	65.00
146	Link Necklace	65.00
147	Link Necklace	65.00
148	Link Necklace	65.00
149	Link Necklace	35.00
150	Link Necklace	65.00
213	Link Necklace	78.00
145	Link Necklace	65.00
113	Link Necklace	75.00
HATPINS		
103	Hatpin	7.00
105	Hatpin	5.00
109	Hatpin	5.50
122	Hatpin	8.50
123	Hatpin	10.00
145	Hatpin	4.50
205	Hatpin	5.50

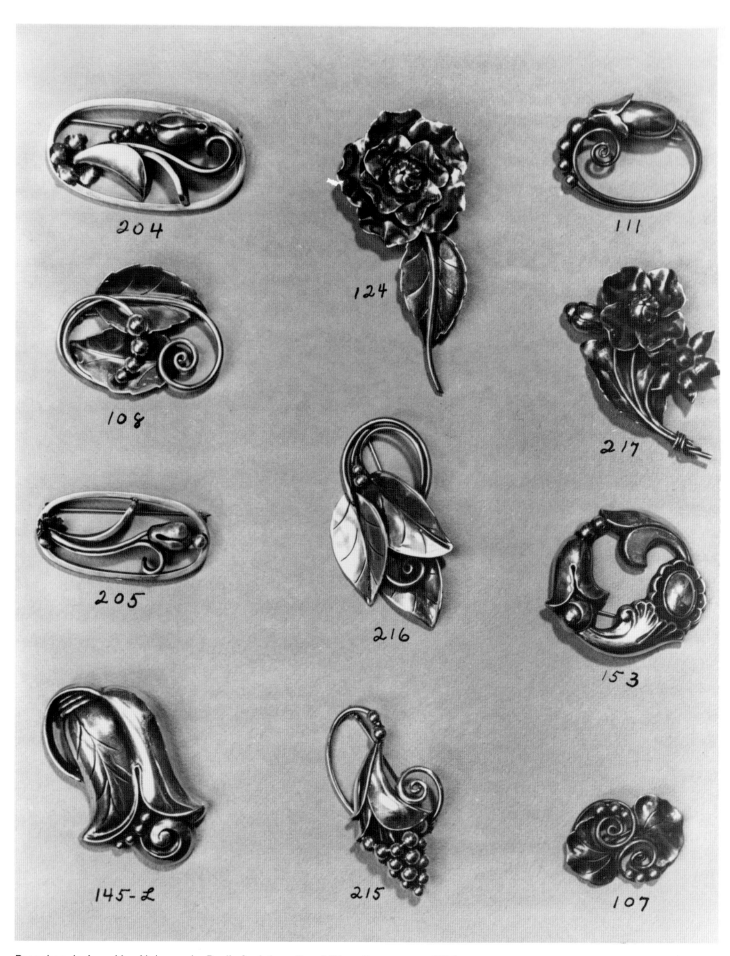

Brooches designed by Alphonse La Paglia for International Silver Company, c. 1952

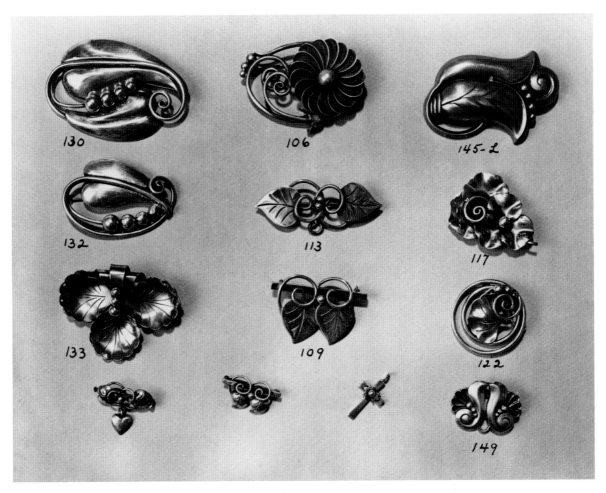

Brooches designed by Alphonse La Paglia for International Silver Company, c. 1952

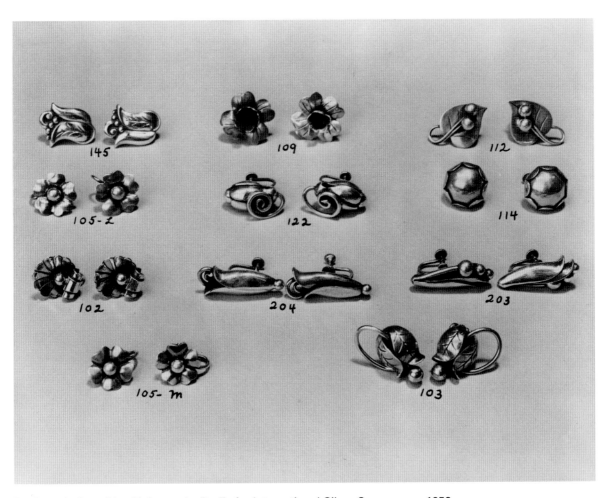

Earrings designed by Alphonse La Paglia for International Silver Company, c. 1952

Cuff bracelet with leaf and berry design by Alphonse La Paglia for International Sterling, c. 1952. 2-3/4", 1-1/2" across design. *Courtesy of Last Century Antiques*

149

102

145

213

100

113

Necklaces designed by Alphonse La Paglia for International Silver Company, c. 1952

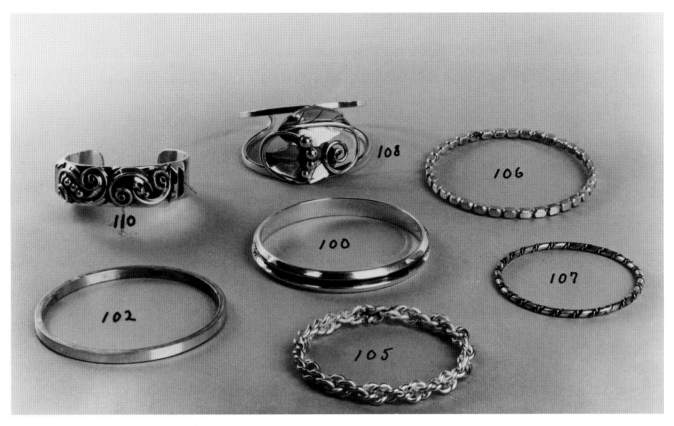

Bangle bracelets designed by Alphonse La Paglia for International Silver Company, c. 1952

Link necklaces and bracelets designed by Alphonse La Paglia for International Silver Company, c. 1952

Link bracelets designed by Alphonse La Paglia for International Silver Company, c. 1952

Link bracelets, brooches, and earrings designed by Alphonse La Paglia for International Silver Company, c. 1952

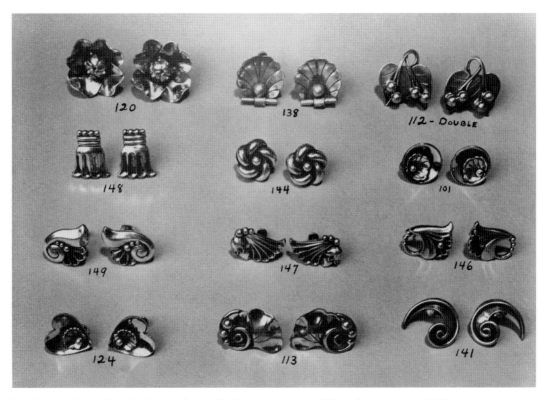

Earrings designed by Alphonse La Paglia for International Silver Company, c. 1952

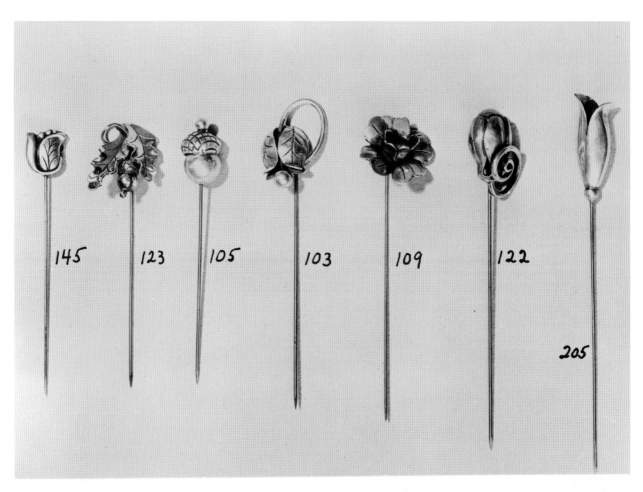

145 123 105 103 109 122

205

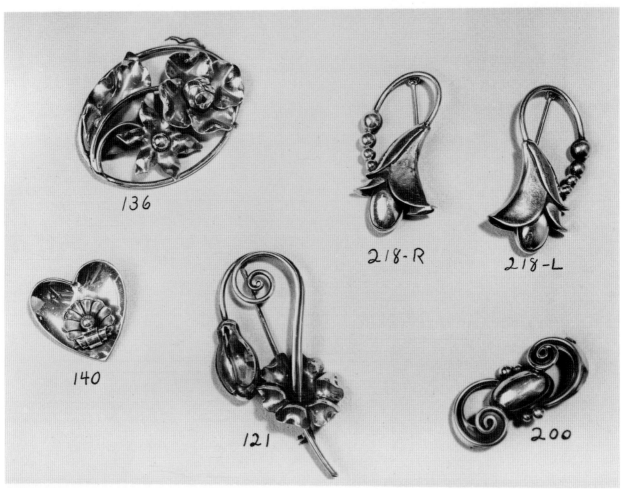

136

218-R 218-L

140 121 200

Stick pins and brooches designed by Alphonse La Paglia for International Silver Company, c. 1952

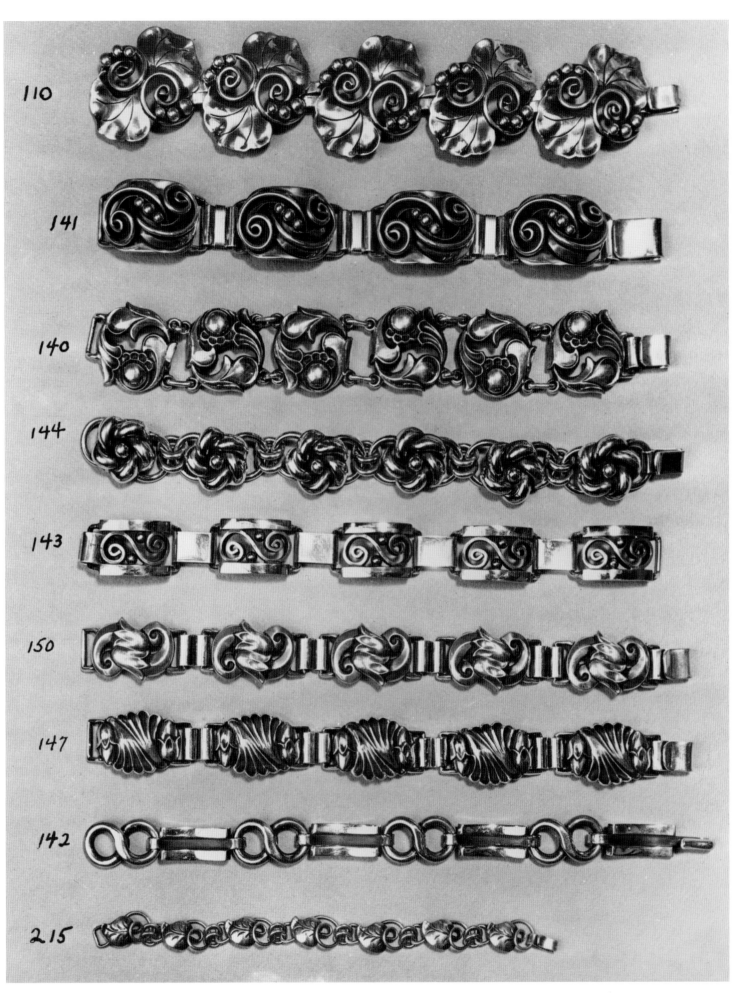

110

141

140

144

143

150

147

142

215

Link bracelets designed by Alphonse La Paglia for International Silver Company, c. 1952

126

207

134

129

210

105

128

211

202

137

210

101

154

140

103

145

Brooches designed by Alphonse La Paglia for International Silver Company, c. 1952

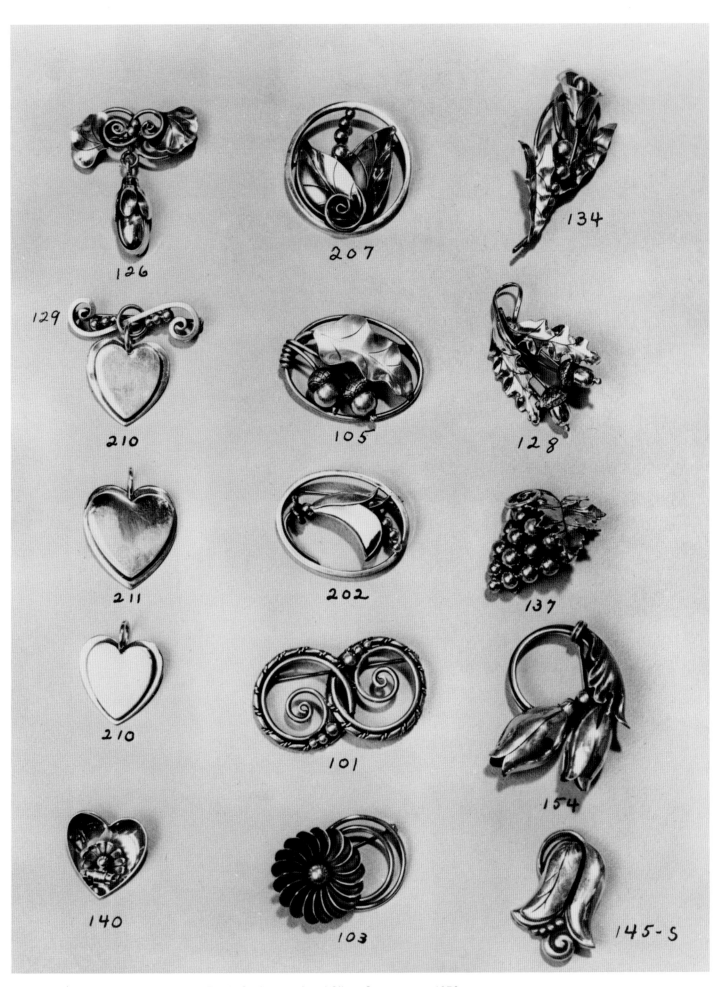

126

207

134

129

210

105

128

211

202

137

210

101

154

140

103

145-S

Brooches designed by Alphonse La Paglia for International Silver Company, c. 1952

Necklace designed by Alphonse La Paglia for International Silver Company, c. 1952, 5.5" diameter. *Courtesy of Dr. Morton & Maidie Kaplon of Summit, New Jersey.*

Bracelet designed by Alphonse La Paglia for International Silver Company, c. 1952, 6.5" long. *Courtesy of Dr. Morton & Maidie Kaplon of Summit, New Jersey.*

International Sterling's 1952 Catalog of Hollowware and Jewelry

International Sterling – La Paglia Designed

RETAIL PRICE LIST
Effective April 2, 1952
(Prices include Federal Excise Tax)

NO.	ITEM	PRICE		NO.	ITEM	PRICE
100	Sauce Ladle	17.00		116	Tea Bell, Medium	65.00
102	Sauce Ladle	17.00		118	Tea Bell, Large	110.00
105	Sauce Ladle	15.00		112	Tea Bell, Small	22.00
106	Sauce Ladle	18.00		119	Table Lighter	65.00
107	Sauce Ladle	18.00		160	Table Lighter	30.00
109	Sauce Ladle	15.00		215	Table Lighter	42.00
100	Jam Spoon	15.00		200	Match Box	17.00
103	Salt Spoon	6.00		120	Stamp Box	32.00
112	Cheese Knife	18.00		112	Cigarette Box	190.00
130	Cheese Knife	20.00		160	Cigarette Container	30.00
112	Pickle Fork	15.00		123	Cigarette Box, Covered	65.00
112	Sugar Spoon	15.00		124	Cigarette Tray	35.00
112	Demi Spoon	8.00		200	Candle Snuffer	32.00
120	Cake Knife	42.00		125	Picture Frame 3¼" x 4¼"	65.00
121	Cake Knife	45.00		126	Picture Frame 5" x 7"	85.00
122	Letter Opener	22.00		127	Picture Frame 8" x 10"	125.00
160	Letter Opener	22.00		200	Baby Cup	48.00
200	Letter Opener	28.00		202	Baby Cup	52.00
204	Letter Opener	28.00		105	Nut Dish	45.00
206	Letter Opener	28.00		117	Nut Dish, Small	30.00
131	Large Ladle	38.00		108	Candy Dish, Covered	110.00
100	Napkin Band	17.00				
101	Napkin Band	17.00		114	Sugar & Cream	185.00
118	Jigger	28.00		130	Coffee Pot	265.00
116	Jigger	30.00			Three Piece Set	450.00

NO.	ITEM	PRICE		NO.	ITEM	PRICE
200	Sugar Bowl	115.00		116	Candlesticks	pr. 140.00
202	Creamer	115.00		118	Candlesticks	pr. 160.00
124	Coffee Pot	310.00		215	Candlesticks	pr. 140.00
124	Tea Pot	310.00		120	Candlesticks	pr. 250.00
				215	Candelabra	pr. 525.00
	Four Piece Set	850.00		121	Candelabra	pr. 350.00
				145	Mint Julep	45.00
				100	Cordial Cup	15.00
151	Bowl, Footed	110.00		102	Cordial Cup	15.00
133	Candy Bowl	50.00		205	Goblet	65.00
114	Bowl	60.00		103	Open Salt	ea. 10.00
116	Fruit Bowl	175.00		113	Salt & Pepper	pr. 70.00
118	Fruit Bowl	200.00		113	Open Salt	ea. 22.00
160	Bowl (Oval)	200.00		147	Salt & Pepper	pr. 70.00
210	Fruit Bowl	150.00		147	Open Salt	ea. 25.00
215	Bowl, Footed	375.00		206	Open Salt	ea. 15.00
200	Punch Bowl	750.00		118S	Compote	65.00
202	Punch Ladle	100.00		137	Compote	110.00
206	Punch Ladle	140.00		116	Vase	160.00
208	Water Pitcher	285.00		115	Tray with handles, oval	140.00
140	Gravy Boat	110.00		114	Tray, no handles, oval	90.00
206	Gravy Boat Tray	65.00		106A	Tray, 17 inch	400.00
146	Butter Boat	65.00		106B	Tray, 20 inch	500.00
220	Pipkin, small	70.00		106C	Tray, 23 inch	650.00
212	Pipkin, large	110.00		133	Tray	200.00
205	Jam Jar	25.00		112	Vegetable Dish, open	140.00
215	Jam Jar	25.00		131	Vegetable Dish, Covered	240.00
215	Sandwich (Footed)	140.00		132	Vegetable Dish, Covered	325.00
108	Bread Tray	140.00		138	Vegetable Dish, Covered	425.00

1952 International Silver catalog of items designed and
made "by the gifted young designer, [Alphonse] La Paglia."
Courtesy of Romance with Silver Collection

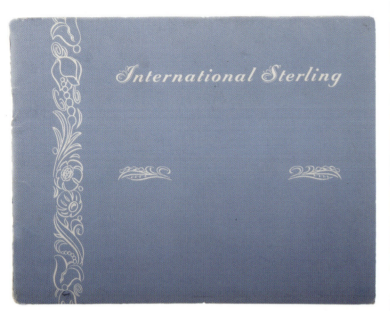

A NEW INTERPRETATION OF BEAUTY ... IN PRECIOUS SOLID SILVER

We are very proud to announce a superb new collection of International Sterling holloware and jewelry—by the gifted young designer, La Paglia.

Here is a truly unusual concept of beauty . . . deep sculptured ornament in natural forms with adventurous shapes of contemporary inspiration.

Perfection in small sizes for the discriminating gift giver. *Left to right—Top:* No. 200 Baby Cup, $48; No. 202 Baby Cup, $52; *Bottom:* No. 215 Jam Jar, $25; No. 100 Jam Spoon, $15; No. 205 Jam Jar, 4 in. high, $25.

Despite the contemporary motifs of these opulent pieces, their vitality seems to echo again the flamboyant spirit of the Renaissance. *Left to right—Top:* No. 108 Covered Candy Dish, $110; No. 118 Compote, 8 in. high, $65; *Bottom:* No. 117 Nut Dish, $30; No. 105 Nut Dish, $45.

Opulent three-dimensional ornament gains tremendous richness from shimmering expanses of unadorned silver. No. 200 Punch Bowl, 13½ in. diameter, $750; *Left:* No. 206 Punch Ladle, $140; *Right:* No. 202 Punch Ladle, $100.

For your home, exquisite bowls, trays, candelabra and many other pieces—all distinguished by a rare use of gleaming surfaces and bold, three-dimensional ornamentation.

And jewelry, too, in arresting motifs that will capture every woman's heart!

We invite you to visit us at your earliest opportunity—to see this beautiful new array of International Sterling—La Paglia designed and executed—in the solid silver with beauty that lives forever.

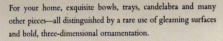

Shapes reminiscent of the traditional, ornament original and contemporary . . . a striking combination. No. 106B Tray, 23½ in. long, $500; No. 124 Tea Pot, $310; No. 124 Coffee Pot, $310; No. 200 Sugar Bowl, $115; No. 202 Creamer, $115. 4-piece set without Tray, $850.

(All Prices include Federal Excise Tax)

Warmth and hospitality are expressed in the wealth of decoration, while the modern forms give exactly the touch of restraint needed. No. 114 Sugar and Cream, $185; No. 130 Coffee Pot, $265; No. 106A Tray, 17 in. long, $400.

These pieces give the feeling they have been carved, like sculpture, from a block of solid silver . . . a wonderfully rich effect. No. 120 Candlesticks, 9¼ in. high, $250 pair; No. 137 Compote, $110.

For sheer poetry of line, these remarkable pieces are unrivaled. *Left to right:* No. 146 Sauce Boat, $65; No. 140 Gravy Boat and Tray, 8 in. long, $175; No. 131 Ladle, $38.

New World motifs . . . pumpkin, seeds, and abstract flower forms . . . are lavishly used to create a feeling of wealth and welcome. No. 215 Footed Bowl, 7¾ in. high, $375; No. 215 Candelabra, $525 pair.

Swirling bell flower, curved bar and ball motifs create harmonizing pieces of rich distinction. No. 118 Compote, $200; No. 121 Candelabra, 8 in. high, $350 pair.

Wealth with simplicity keynotes this matching set for hors d'oeuvres and after-dinner use. No. 112 Demi-Tasse Spoons, $8 each; No. 112 Sugar Spoon, Cheese Knife and Pickle Fork, $15, $18 and $15 respectively.

The luxurious beauty of these sterling drinking vessels prepares the palate for absolute perfection. *Left to right:* No. 100 Cordial Cup, 3 in. high, $15; No. 116 Jigger, $30; No. 145 Mint Julep (also highballs, Collins, etc.), $45; No. 118 Jigger, $28; No. 102 Cordial Cup, $15.

Symmetry of form, perfectly balanced proportion and the striking use of opulent ornament have combined to produce one of the most outstanding examples of contemporary silver. No. 215 Footed Bowl, 7¾ in. high, $375.

Magnificent hand-worked table appointments. Lighter mechanism takes standard Evans parts. *Left to right:* No. 119 Table Lighter, 3¼ in. high, $65; No. 215 Table Lighter, $42; No. 160 Table Lighter, $30; No. 200 Candle Snuffer, $32.

Accessories which couple individuality with superb taste. *Left to right—Top:* No. 112 Cigarette Box, 6½ in. long, $190; No. 123 Cigarette Box, $65; *Bottom:* No. 124 Cigarette Tray, $35; No. 200 Match Box, $17.

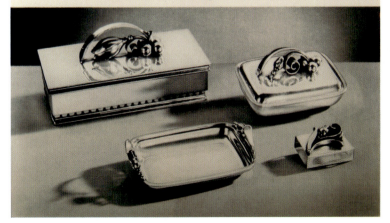

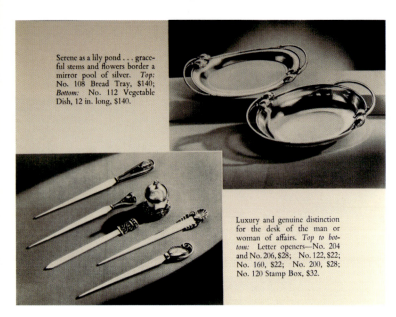

Serene as a lily pond . . . graceful stems and flowers border a mirror pool of silver. *Top:* No. 108 Bread Tray, $140; *Bottom:* No. 112 Vegetable Dish, 12 in. long, $140.

Luxury and genuine distinction for the desk of the man or woman of affairs. *Top to bottom:* Letter openers—No. 204 and No. 206, $28; No. 122, $22; No. 160, $22; No. 200, $28; No. 120 Stamp Box, $32.

Necklaces in rich, three-dimensional modern forms· . . . $65 to $78.

Matching ensemble of bracelets, necklace, brooch, earrings, stickpin . . . for someone special . . . $7 to $65.

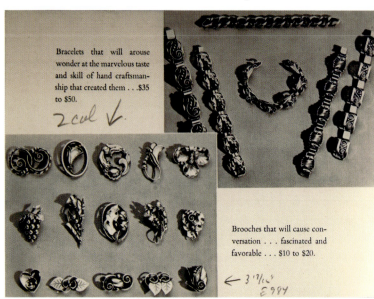

Bracelets that will arouse wonder at the marvelous taste and skill of hand craftsmanship that created them . . .$35 to $50.

Brooches that will cause conversation . . . fascinated and favorable . . . $10 to $20.

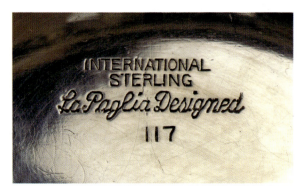

A small dish on a floral base, made by Alphonse La Paglia. 3.25" x 3.25" x 1.25". *Courtesy of Dr. Morton & Maidie Kaplon of Summit, New Jersey*

International Sterling Craft Associates Catalogs, 1954

1954 *International Sterling Craft Associates* brochure presenting "a superb collection of Sterling Hollowware and Jewelry – La Paglia Designed." *Courtesy of Romance with Silver Collection*

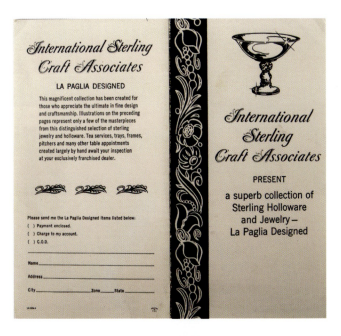

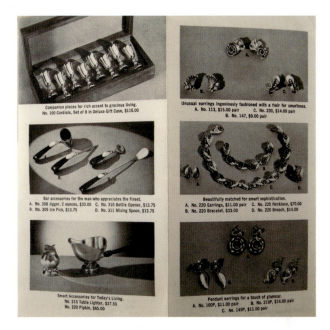

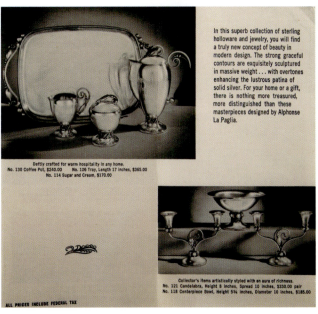

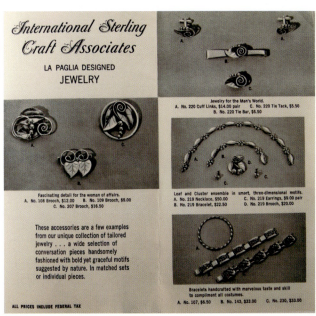

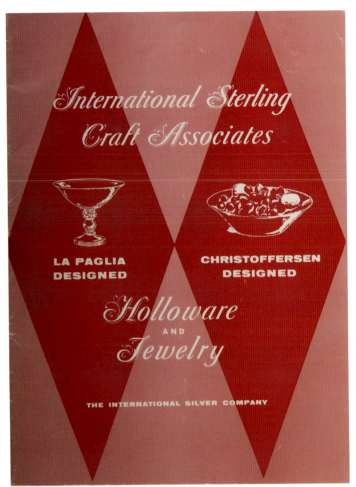

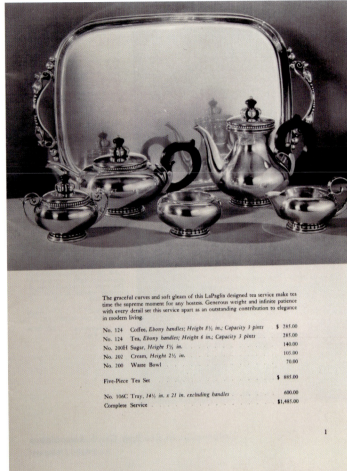

The graceful curves and soft gleam of this LaPaglia designed tea service make tea time the supreme moment for any hostess. Generous weight and infinite patience with every detail set this service apart as an outstanding contribution to elegance in modern living.

No. 124	Coffee, *Ebony handles; Height 8½ in.; Capacity 3 pints*	$ 285.00
No. 124	Tea, *Ebony handles; Height 6 in.; Capacity 3 pints*	285.00
No. 200H	Sugar, *Height 5½ in.*	140.00
No. 202	Cream, *Height 2½ in.*	105.00
No. 200	Waste Bowl	70.00
	Five-Piece Tea Set	$ 885.00
No. 106C	Tray, *14½ in. x 21 in. excluding handles*	600.00
	Complete Service	$1,485.00

1

LaPaglia Designed

Sterling of collection calibre for those who fully appreciate the finest. It combines a mastery of contemporary design with a Renaissance flair for rich ornamentation . . . bold sculptured motifs drawn from nature to enrich the gleaming silver surfaces forever.

All pieces are individually crafted and characterized by extremely massive weight and lustrous patina. For the home or as a gift, there is nothing you can choose more imaginative in concept or lovelier in execution than LaPaglia Designed sterling. It will be admired and treasured for generations.

International Sterling

The graceful simplicity of the body rests lightly on an exquisitely detailed floral gallery. Matching in elegance is the tulip inspired hand-carved ebony handle with curving flower tendril. The flower pod finial pours a graceful rhythm of seeds suggesting copious hospitality. The whole impression is one of great wealth restrained by good taste.

No. 130	Coffee Pot *Height 9 in.*	$240.00
No. 114	Sugar and Cream *Set,*	170.00
	3-Piece Set	$410.00
No. 106	Tray *10½ in. x 15 in. excluding handles*	365.00
	Complete Service	$775.00

In these lovely pieces . . . part of the superb collection of International Sterling designed by LaPaglia . . . strong graceful lines blend with restrained three dimensional ornament to capture every woman's heart.

No. 116	Bowl *Diameter 10 in.; Height 5½ in.*	$160.00
No. 116	Candlesticks *Height 4 in.*	Pair, 125.00

2

International Sterling Craft Associates
La Paglia Designed

LaPaglia in its richest design. Opulent ornament achieves a vigor and flamboyance reminiscent of the early Renaissance. Shapes are completely modern. Exuberant use of natural motifs ... seed, tendril and pumpkin ... express the robust vitality and growth always present in nature. Few modern silversmiths will attempt work requiring such skill.

No. 215 Centerpiece Bowl $350.00
Diameter 10 in.; Height 7¼ in.

No. 215 Candelabra   *Pair*,   480.00
Removable arms; Height 8¼ in.;
Spread 10½ in.

No. 215 Candlesticks only *Pair*,   125.00
(without arms)

The addition of a floral gallery to the three dimensional ornament recommends this design to those who prefer greater detail of ornament.

No. 118 Bowl $185.00
Diameter 10 in.; Height 5¾ in.

No. 118 Candlesticks   *Pair*,   145.00
Height 4¼ in.

International Sterling Craft Associates
La Paglia Designed   3

Festivity in the grand manner ... Truly the punch bowl is the center of entertainment, the very well of hospitality. For those who entertain magnificently, here is the supreme gift. Picture this capacious punch bowl with its lavish base expressing the abundance of nature frosted and coolly shimmering on your buffet.

No. 200 Punch Bowl $735.00
Diameter 14½ in.; Height 7¾
in.; Capacity 24 pints to brim

No. 206 Punch Ladle   125.00
Length 13½ in.

For melted butter, syrup, chocolate sauce, mint jelly, gravy or cream — and lovely as a flower holder — this sauce boat is a choice example of contemporary craftsmanship.

No. 146 Sauce Boat $60.00
Length 6 in.; Height 3¾ in.

No. 102 Ladle   15.00

International Sterling Craft Associates
La Paglia Designed   5

LaPaglia created more than a beautiful design in his sterling, its beauty expresses a poetic idea as well. Here in these candelabra, the base represents the earth. Growing from it, spherical and tubular forms symbolize flower bulbs and roots. From these spring graceful stems which hold aloft flowers ripe with seeds, ready to drop to earth and begin again the cycle of life.

No. 121 Candelabra   *Pair*, $330.00
Height 8 in.; Spread 10 in.

Only a matchless feeling for good design could create pieces as incredibly rich and ornate, yet somehow so simple. A remarkable feat of artistry in sterling, these pieces are at home anywhere.

No. 120 Candle Holders *Pair*, $225.00
Height 9¼ in.

4   **International Sterling Craft Associates**
                    La Paglia Designed

The unaffected flow of line makes these tendril handles seem to grow from the silver itself. Each piece is crafted in heavy weight sterling with a pleasing harmony of line.

No. 108 Bread or Roll Tray $125.00
Overall length 13 in.

No. 112 Vegetable Dish   125.00
Overall length 11¼ in.

These bowls offer a wide variety of uses — for sauces, mints, candy, nuts, jellies or flowers. But their charm also lies in their decorative qualities which make them treasures of the future.

Left to right:

No. 133 Sauce Bowl $ 45.00
Diameter 5 in.; Height 2¾ in.

No. 151 Sauce Bowl   100.00
Diameter 5¼ in.; Height 5 in.

No. 114 Sauce Bowl   55.00
Diameter 5¼ in.; Height 3¼ in.

6   **International Sterling Craft Associates**
                    La Paglia Designed

These are truly collector's items, to be possessed and treasured through the years. Symmetry of form, perfectly balanced proportion and striking use of opulent ornament make these pieces striking examples of contemporary silver.

No. 160 Table Lighter $27.50
Height 2 in.

No. 118S Compote   60.00
Diameter 5¼ in.;
Height 3½ in.

No. 123 Cigarette Box; Small   60.00
4 in. x 3 in.

Contemporary design in heavy sterling. Treasured pictures of loved ones are fittingly cherished in this exquisitely fashioned sterling silver picture frame. Imagine grandmother's delight with baby's portrait in this charming LaPaglia creation.

No. 126 Frame *Approximately 5 in. x 7 in.* $75.00

New splendor for your table . . . a gleaming sterling water pitcher designed by LaPaglia. Rare in its pure design and perfect balance, this pitcher will harmonize with all accessories.

No. 208 Pitcher $260.00
Height 8¼ in.; Capacity 4 pints

8   **International Sterling Craft Associates**
La Paglia Designed

The Mint Julep in heavy sterling serves many purposes — whether for iced tea, highballs or as a practical vase. Its subtly flaring shape is a triumph of design.

Two-way jiggers of one ounce and two ounce capacity will flatter a gentleman's taste in more ways than one.

No. 118 Double Jigger $25.00
Height 3½ in.

No. 145 Mint Julep or   *Each,* 40.00
Highball
Height 5⅜ in.

No. 116 Double Jigger   27.50
Height 3½ in.

No. 100 Cordial   *Each,* 13.75
Height 3¼ in.

For the gift to friends who "have everything", these cordial cups are a symbol of perfection. You will want to collect a set of your own for those special quiet moments with coffee, cordial and candlelight.

No. LH37-100 Set of 8 $116.00
Cordial Cups, *Gift Boxed*

International Sterling Craft Associates   7
La Paglia Designed

Ingeniously fashioned to accent the rich beauty of solid silver, this lovely reflecting tray is useful in many ways. A conversation piece, it's a perfect setting for sugar and cream set, hors d'oeuvres, cocktails or a pair of champagne glasses.

No. 115 Oval Tray with handles $125.00
Length overall 10¼ in.

All of these pieces are fashioned with deft imagination — works of art to become prized possessions for someone who appreciates the ultimate in fine design.

No. 112 Cigarette Box $175.00
Length 6½ in.; Width 3¼ in.

No. 105 Nut Dish, large $41.25
Length 5 in.

No. 117 Nut Dish $27.50
Length 3¼ in.

No. 206 Nut Dish,   *Each,* $13.75
Individual
Diameter 2 in.

International Sterling Craft Associates   9
La Paglia Designed

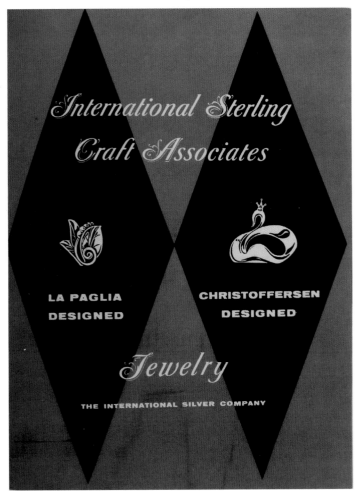

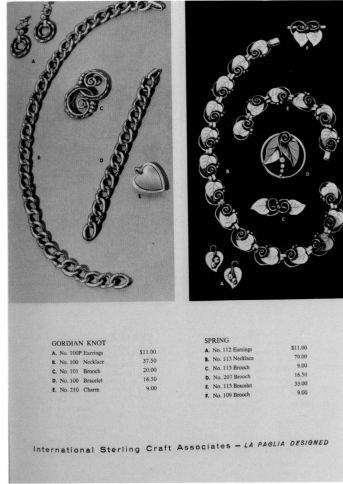

GORDIAN KNOT			SPRING		
A.	No. 100P Earrings	$11.00	A.	No. 112 Earrings	$11.00
B.	No. 100 Necklace	37.50	B.	No. 113 Necklace	70.00
C.	No. 101 Brooch	20.00	C.	No. 113 Brooch	9.00
D.	No. 100 Bracelet	16.50	D.	No. 207 Brooch	16.50
E.	No. 210 Charm	9.00	E.	No. 113 Bracelet	33.00
			F.	No. 109 Brooch	9.00

International Sterling Craft Associates — *LA PAGLIA DESIGNED*

LaPaglia Designed

To those who appreciate only the finest, we're proud to present this unusual collection of stunning jewelry in precious sterling . . . sparkling designs with bold sculptured motifs as timeless as nature . . . all interpreted with graceful movement . . . superbly crafted by master silversmiths. Whether it's an individual piece or matched set, International Sterling — LaPaglia Designed jewelry is truly sterling of collection calibre to be treasured through many generations.

International Sterling

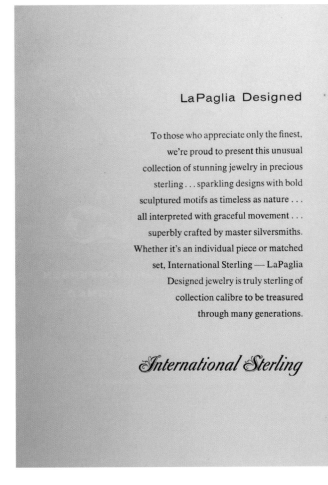

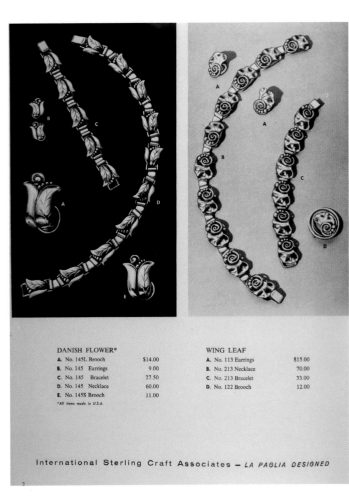

DANISH FLOWER*			WING LEAF		
A.	No. 145L Brooch	$14.00	A.	No. 113 Earrings	$15.00
B.	No. 145 Earrings	9.00	B.	No. 213 Necklace	70.00
C.	No. 145 Bracelet	27.50	C.	No. 213 Bracelet	33.00
D.	No. 145 Necklace	60.00	D.	No. 122 Brooch	12.00
E.	No. 145S Brooch	11.00			

*All items made in U.S.A.

International Sterling Craft Associates — *LA PAGLIA DESIGNED*

LEAF AND BLOSSOM (above left)
- A. No. 219 Necklace — $50.00
- B. No. 219P Earrings — 14.00
- C. No. 219 Brooch — 20.00
- D. No. 219 Bracelet — 22.50

SEEDS (bottom left)
- A. No. 220 Necklace — $70.00
- B. No. 220 Brooch — 14.00
- C. No. 220 Bracelet — 33.00
- D. No. 220 Earrings — 11.00

BUD (above right)
- A. No. 102 Necklace — $60.00
- B. No. 102 Bracelet — 33.00
- C. No. 103 Earrings — 14.00

OAK (bottom right)
- A. No. 123 Earrings — $14.00
- B. No. 125 Bracelet — 33.00
- C. No. 128 Brooch — 14.00

International Sterling Craft Associates — *LA PAGLIA DESIGNED*

3

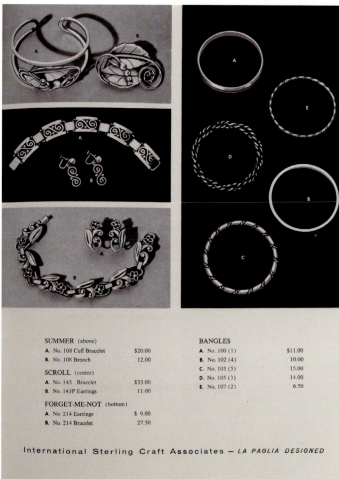

SUMMER (above)
- A. No. 108 Cuff Bracelet — $20.00
- B. No. 108 Brooch — 12.00

SCROLL (center)
- A. No. 143 Bracelet — $33.00
- B. No. 143P Earrings — 11.00

FORGET-ME-NOT (bottom)
- A. No. 214 Earrings — $ 9.00
- B. No. 214 Bracelet — 27.50

BANGLES
- A. No. 100 (1) — $11.00
- B. No. 102 (4) — 10.00
- C. No. 103 (5) — 15.00
- D. No. 105 (3) — 14.00
- E. No. 107 (2) — 6.50

International Sterling Craft Associates — *LA PAGLIA DESIGNED*

5

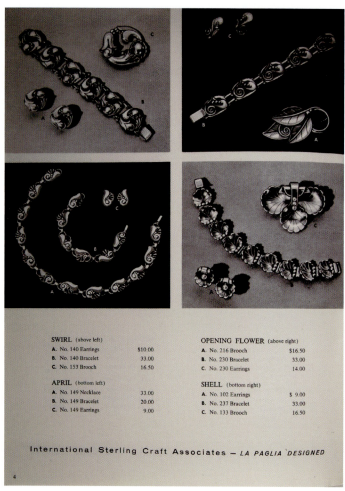

SWIRL (above left)
- A. No. 140 Earrings — $10.00
- B. No. 140 Bracelet — 33.00
- C. No. 153 Brooch — 16.50

APRIL (bottom left)
- A. No. 149 Necklace — 33.00
- B. No. 149 Bracelet — 20.00
- C. No. 149 Earrings — 9.00

OPENING FLOWER (above right)
- A. No. 216 Brooch — $16.50
- B. No. 230 Bracelet — 33.00
- C. No. 230 Earrings — 14.00

SHELL (bottom right)
- A. No. 102 Earrings — $ 9.00
- B. No. 237 Bracelet — 33.00
- C. No. 133 Brooch — 16.50

International Sterling Craft Associates — *LA PAGLIA DESIGNED*

4

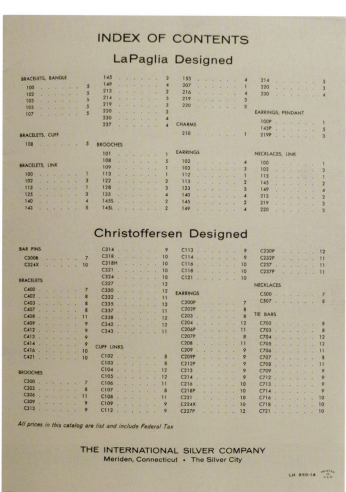

INDEX OF CONTENTS

LaPaglia Designed

Christoffersen Designed

All prices in this catalog are list and include Federal Tax

THE INTERNATIONAL SILVER COMPANY
Meriden, Connecticut • The Silver City

LH 958-14

International Sterling La Paglia Designed

Footed vegetable #243 designed by Alphonse La Paglia for International Silver and marked *La Paglia Designed,* c. 1952. 10 ¾" x 7 ¾" x 3" high. *Courtesy of Romance with Silver Collection*

Various footed bowls, a goblet, and a sugar shaker designed by Alphonse La Paglia for International Silver Company, c. 1952

Two footed bowls designed by Alphonse La Paglia for International Silver Company, c. 1952

Two bowls and two service dishes designed by Alphonse La Paglia for International Silver Company, c. 1952

Two deep oval bowls designed by Alphonse La Paglia for International Silver Company, c. 1952. Large #233, 9" x 6 ¾" X 5 ¼" tall; Small #232, 7" x 5 ¼" x 4 1/8" tall. *Courtesy of Romance with Silver Collection*

Two small pedestal bowls, #139/40 and #118, designed by Alphonse La Paglia for International Silver Company, 1952. Left: 3 ½" x 5" high; right: 3 ¼" x 3 7/8". *Courtesy of Romance with Silver Collection*

INTERNATIONAL STERLING
La Paglia Designed
139   40

INTERNATIONAL STERLING
La Paglia Designed
118

Console set of a bowl and two candelabras designed by Alphonse La Paglia. Bowl #139/14 made for International Silver Company, 1952, 10" d. x 5" h; and candelabra #121, 7 5/8" wide x 10" high. *Courtesy of Romance with Silver Collection*

Large bowl #139/35-1 designed by Alphonse La Paglia for International Silver Company, 1952, 10" diameter, 6" high. *Courtesy of Romance with Silver Collection*

Footed bowl #133 designed by Alphonse La Paglia for
International Silver Company, c. 1952, 3 1/8" x 4 7/8" high.
Courtesy of Romance with Silver Collection

Candlesticks designed by Alphonse La Paglia for International Silver Company, c. 1952

Bowl and candlesticks designed by Alphonse La Paglia for International
Silver Company, c. 1952

Console set including candlestick #118 designed by Alphonse
La Paglia for International Silver Company, c. 1952. 4 5/8", and
bowl #118 made by Alphonse La Paglia. 5.75" x 10". *Courtesy
of Romance with Silver Collection*

Pair of candlesticks #120 designed by Alphonse La Paglia for International Silver Company, c. 1952, 9 3/8" high x 3 5/8" diam. *Courtesy of Romance with Silver Collection*

A 2-arm candelabra designed by Alphonse La Paglia for International Silver Company, c. 1952.

Covered box #112 designed by Alphonse La Paglia for International Silver Company, c. 1952, 6 3/8" x 3 1/4" x 2 3/4" high. *Courtesy of Romance with Silver Collection*

Lighter designed by Alphonse La Paglia for International Sterling Company, c. 1952, 3" tall x 2" diameter

A smoking set, including a covered cigarette box, two ash trays, a lighter, and a match holder, each designed by Alphonse La Paglia for International Silver Company, c. 1952

INTERNATIONAL STERLING
La Paglia Designed
118

4-tiered server #118 designed by Alphonse La Paglia for International Silver Company, c. 1952. Bottom tier 11" d x 5" h; middle tier 9" x 4 ½" h; upper tier 7 1/8" x 4"; top bowl 3 ¾" x 3" high. *Courtesy of Romance with Silver Collection*

A footed compote designed by Alphonse La Paglia for International Silver Company, c. 1952

INTERNATIONAL
STERLING
La Paglia Designed
137

Pedestal dish
#137 designed by
Alphonse La Paglia
for International Silver
Company, c. 1952, 7 ½"
diam., 6" high. *Courtesy
of Romance with Silver
Collection*

INTERNATIONAL
STERLING
La Paglia Designed
215

Two large compotes designed by
Alphonse La Paglia for International
Silver Company, c. 1952, 10" d x 8"
h. Left marked #215, right marked
#215x. *Courtesy of Romance with
Silver Collection*

Sherbet #118 designed by Alphonse La Paglia for International Silver Company, c. 1952, part of a boxed set, 4" diameter x 3 1/3" tall. *Courtesy of Romance with Silver Collection*

Small, medium, and large goblets for cordial, wine, and water, each designed by Alphonse La Paglia for International Silver Company, c. 1952

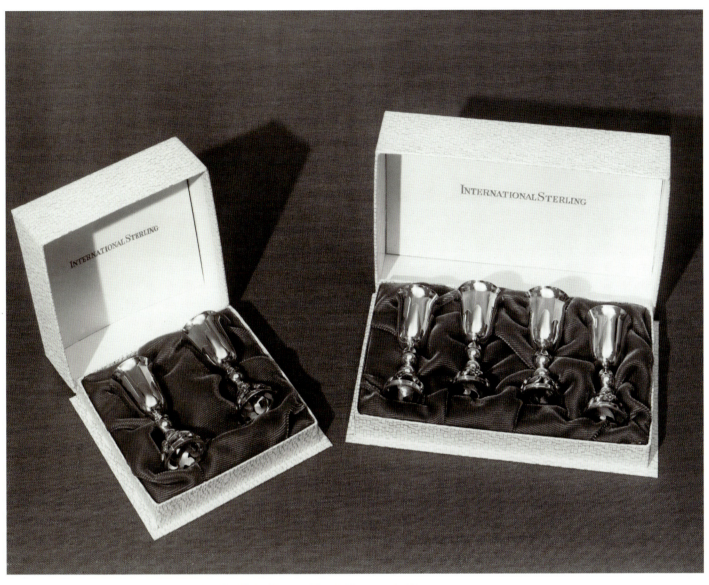

Wine goblets designed by Alphonse La Paglia for International Silver, c. 1952, presented in gift boxes

Set of six goblets #139-50 designed by Alphonse La Paglia for International Silver Company, c. 1952, each 6.5" high. *Courtesy of Romance with Silver Collection*

Cordial cups #139 25 designed by
Alphonse La Paglia for International
Silver Company, c. 1952, in a
presentation box, each cup 3" high.
*Courtesy of Romance with Silver
Collection*

Tray #115 and 8 cordials #100 designed by Alphonse La Paglia for International Silver Company, c. 1952. Cordials 3 1/8", tray 10 ½" x 6 ½". *Courtesy of Romance with Silver Collection*

Sherbet cups designed by Alphonse La Paglia for International Silver Company, c. 1952, presented in a gift box. *Courtesy of Romance with Silver Collection*

Trumpet flute cups designed by Alphonse La Paglia for International Silver Company, c. 1952, presented in a gift box. *Courtesy of Romance with Silver Collection*

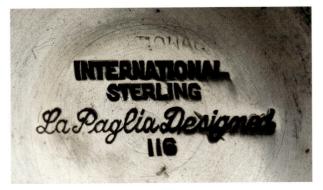

Two jiggers #116 and #139 98-1 designed by Alphonse La Paglia for International. Silver Company, c. 1952. Left: 3 ¾" high, right 3 ½" high. *Courtesy of Romance with Silver Collection*

Shot cups and a julep cup designed by Alphonse La Paglia for International Silver Company, c. 1952

Demitasse saucer and cup holder #118 designed by Alphonse La Paglia for International Silver Company, . 1952, with a ceramic liner. Overall height 3", saucer diameter 4". Part of a boxed set. *Courtesy of Romance with Silver Collection*

Demitasse cups designed by Alphonse La Paglia for International Silver Company, c. 1952, housed in a presentation box. *Courtesy of Romance with Silver Collection*

A baby's cup, a footed cup, and a glass condiment bowl with a silver lid and a spoon, each designed by Alphonse La Paglia for International Silver Company, c. 1952

Set of four cups #17030-5 designed by Alphonse La Paglia for International Silver Copmpany, c. 1952, 4 ½" wide, 3" high. *Courtesy of Romance with Silver Collection*

Salt and pepper shakers, salt cellars, and napkin rings, each designed by Alphonse La Paglia for International Silver Company, c. 1952

Two peppers #147 designed by Alphonse La Paglia, and two salts #147 designed by La Paglia for International Silver Company, c. 1952, with spoons designed by Alphonse La Paglia. Peppers, 4 5/8"; salts, 2" high x 2 1/4". *Courtesy of Romance with Silver Collection*

Two covered sugar bowls, each designed by Alphonse La Paglia for International Silver Company, c. 1952

130

134   6 1/2 x 5 1/2 Hi

Two covered scalloped candy dishes designed by Alphonse La Paglia for
International Silver Company, c. 1952

A small and a large dinner bell, a small covered dish, and a footed dish, each
designed by Alphonse La Paglia for International Silver Company, c. 1952

Two large platters designed by Alphonse La Paglia for International Silver Company, c. 1952. Smaller #170 31/5, 13" diameter; larger #170 25/3, 17" diameter. *Courtesy of Romance with Silver Collection*

Small round plate #139 88 designed by Alphonse La Paglia for International Silver Company, c. 1952, 6 ½" diameter. *Courtesy of Romance with Silver Collection*

Sauce boat #146 designed by Alphonse La Paglia for International Silver Company, c. 1952, 5 ½" x 3 7/8". *Courtesy of Romance with Silver Collection*

Vegetable dish #134 or 194 (?) designed by Alphonse La Paglia
for International Silver Company, c. 1952, 11″ x 6 ½″ x 2 ½″ high.
Courtesy of Romance with Silver Collection

Handled sauce boat #220 designed by Alphonse La Paglia for International Silver Company, c. 1952, 5.25" overall, boat 4.25" wide x 3" high. *Courtesy of Romance with Silver Collection*

Gravy boat and an oval stand, each designed by Alphonse La Paglia for International Silver Company, c. 1952

A water pitcher designed by Alphonse La Paglia for International Silver Company, c. 1952

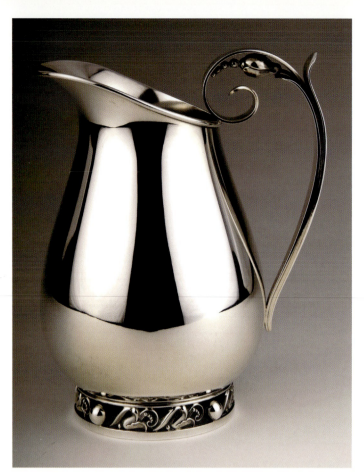

INTERNATIONAL STERLING
La Paglia Designed
118

Water pitcher #118 designed by Alphonse La Paglia for International Silver Company, c. 1952. 8 ½" tall. *Courtesy of Romance with Silver Collection*

A 4-piece coffee service designed by Alphonse La Paglia for International Silver Company, c. 1952, including a coffee pot 9" high, a covered sugar bowl 4" high, a cream pitcher, and a tray 17" long x 10 ½" wide.

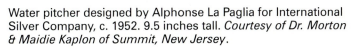

Water pitcher designed by Alphonse La Paglia for International Silver Company, c. 1952. 9.5 inches tall. *Courtesy of Dr. Morton & Maidie Kaplon of Summit, New Jersey*.

Coffee set #114, with a coffee pot, covered sugar, creamer, and tray #139-90 designed by Alphonse La Paglia for International Silver Company, c. 1952. Coffee pot, 9" high, creamer and sugar 4.75" high, tray 10" deep x 17" long. The cream pitcher is also shown separately in a presentation box. *Courtesy of Romance with Silver Collection*

INTERNATIONAL
STERLING
La Paglia Designed

139-90

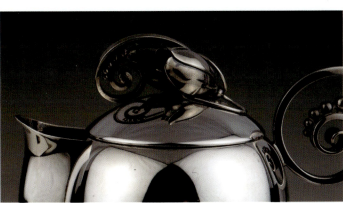

6-piece tea set designed by Alphonse La Paglia for International Silver Company, c. 1952. Tray #106C, 24" x 15"; coffee pot 8 ¾" tall; teapot #124, 6" tall; cream 3 ¾" tall; sugar 4 ¾" tall; waste bowl 2 ¾" tall. *Courtesy of Romance with Silver Collection*

INTERNATIONAL
STERLING
La Paglia Designed
106C

INTERNATIONAL
STERLING
La Paglia Designed
124

A cream pitcher and a covered sugar bowl resting on a small oval tray, each designed by Alphonse La Paglia for International Silver Company, c. 1952.

A 7-piece tea service designed by Alphonse La Paglia for International Silver Company, c. 1952

A 4-piece tea service made by Alphonse La Paglia for International Silver Company, c. 1952

A sugar bowl with a lid and a matching cream pitcher, each made by Alphonse La Paglia for International Silver Company, c. 1952

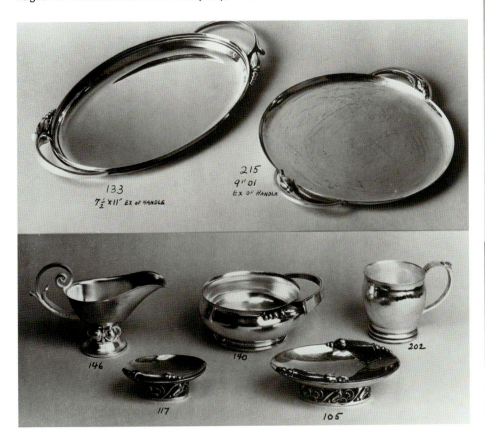

Top row: an oval tray and a round tray
Bottom row: a gravy boat, a sugar bowl and matching cream pitcher, and two footed dishes, each designed by Alphonse La Paglia for International Silver Company, c. 1952

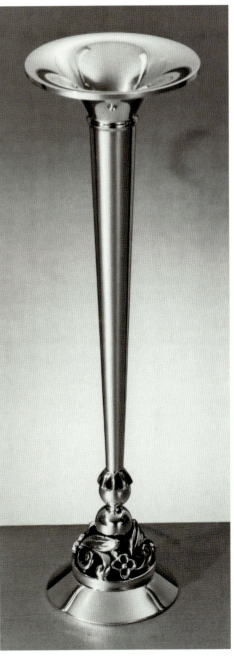

A tall trumpet-shaped vase made by Alphonse La Paglia for International Silver Company, circa 1952.

Tall vase #118 designed by Alphonse La Paglia for International Silver Company, c. 1952, 9 1/4" high x 4 1/4" wide x 4" deep. *Courtesy of Romance with Silver Collection*

A square tray designed by Alphonse La Paglia for International Silver Company, c. 1952

Tray or low vegetable dish #115 designed by Alphonse La Paglia for International Silver Company, c. 1952, 11 ¾" x 6 ½" x 1 ½" high. *Courtesy of Romance with Silver Collection*

A picture frame and two letter openers, each designed by Alphonse La Paglia for International Silver Company, c. 1952

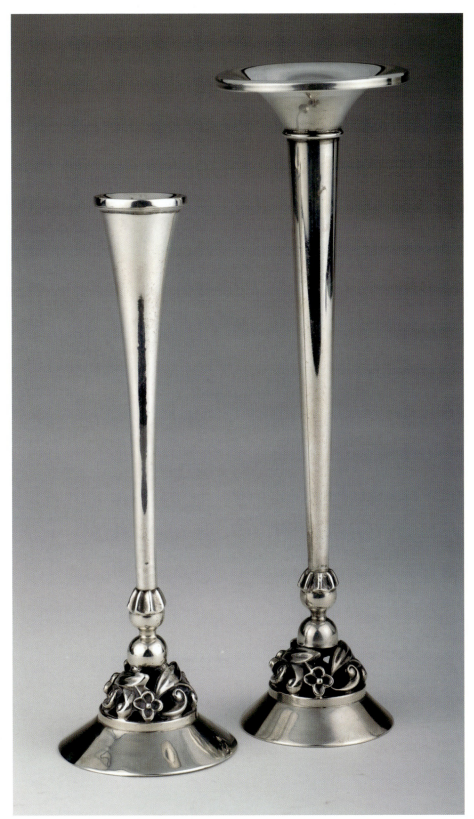

Two bud vases #139 15/2 and #139 66 designed by Alphonse La Paglia for International Silver Company, c. 1952, 6" high & 7"high. *Courtesy of Romance with Silver Collection*

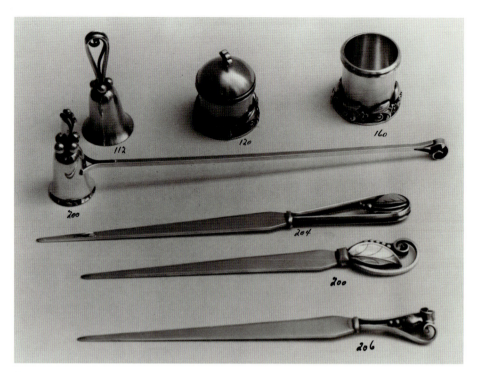

Two dinner bells, two condiment servers, a candle snuff, and three letter openers, all designed by Alphonse La Paglia for International Silver Company, c. 1952

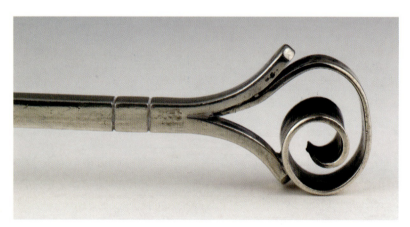

Candle snuffer #200 designed by Alphonse La Paglia for International Silver Company, c. 1952. 11.5" long. *Courtesy of Romance with Silver Collection*

Letter opener with shell end designed by Alphonse La Paglia for International Silver Company, c. 1952, 7 7/8" long. *Courtesy of Romance with Silver Collection*

Two serving utensils designed by Alphonse La Paglia for International Silver Company, c. 1952; fork #301 and spatula #307, each 8" long. *Courtesy of Romance with Silver Collection*

A pair of condiment cellars with spoons, and four serving utensils, each designed by Alphonse La Paglia for International Silver Company, c. 1952

Tart servers and a shoe horn, each designed by Alphonse La Paglia for International Silver Company, c. 1952

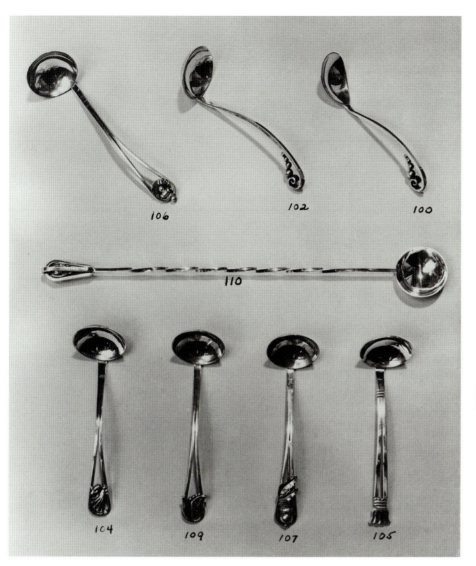

Ladles designed by Alphonse La Paglia for International Silver Company, c. 1952

Ladle #107 designed by Alphonse La Paglia for International Silver Company, c. 1952, 6" long. *Courtesy of Romance with Silver Collection*

Punch ladle #304 designed
by Alphonse La Paglia for
International Silver Company,
c. 1952, 13 ½" long. *Courtesy
of Romance with Silver
Collection*

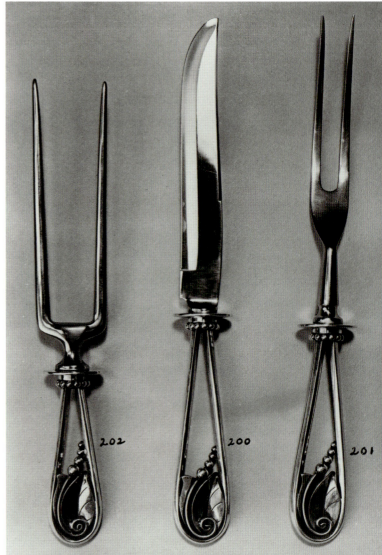

A sharpening fork, a carving knife, and a carving fork, each
designed by Alphonse La Paglia for International Silver
Company, c. 1952

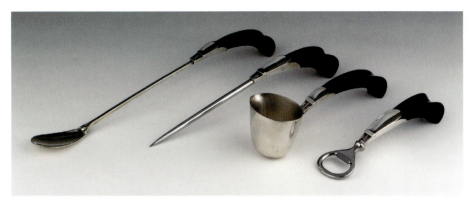

Bar set: stirrer, ice pick, jigger, and bottle opener, each designed by Alphonse La Paglia for International Silver Company, c. 1952. Stirrer 11 ¾" long. *Courtesy of Romance with Silver Collection*

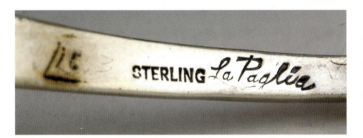

Serving spoon designed by Alphonse La Paglia for International Silver Company, c. 1952. *Courtesy of Romance with Silver Collection*

Various serving utensils, each designed by Alphonse La Paglia for International Silver Company, c. 1952

William G. deMatteo and His Heirs

As the popularity of Danish modern and American colonial silver styles evolved internationally during the 1950s, William G. deMatteo continued to make silver items and to fill commissions for his customers from his workshop in Bergenfield, New Jersey.

The Jensen-inspired items in deMatteo's design book run the gamut from nearly identical reproductions of Jensen design to wholly original designs in the Jensen style. DeMatteo's #46 tea and coffee service, for example, is almost indistinguishable from Jensen's famous no. 2 service.

4-piece tea set # 46, with ivory pistol handles, including hot water pot, tea pot, cream pitcher, and tray, made by William G. deMatteo. *Courtesy of Chip deMatteo*

5-piece tea set #46, with ivory pistol handles, including a hot water pot, tea pot, covered sugar bowl, cream pitcher, and tray, made by William G. deMatteo. *Courtesy of Chip deMatteo*

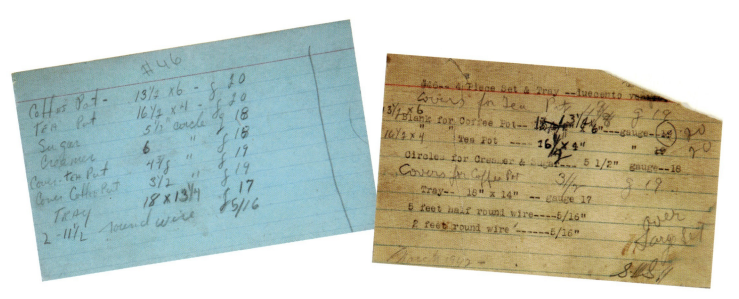

William G. deMatteo's record card for #46 tea service, circa pre-1948. *Courtesy of Chip deMatteo*

William G. deMatteo's record card for #46 4-piece [tea] Set & Tray—luecento. *Courtesy of Chip deMatteo*

Georg Jensen's no. 80 tea set surely inspired deMatteo's design for his #48 tea set, as well as his "#49 Danish tea service," as described on his design record cards.

Tea and coffee set, no. 80, designed by Georg Jensen and made in Copenhagen at the Georg Jensen A/S workshops, inscribed and dated 1934.

3-piece #48 tea set made by William G. deMatteo. *Courtesy of Chip deMatteo*

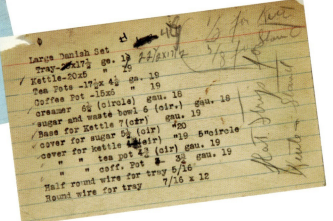

William G. deMatteo's record card for his #48, 3-piece Tea Set. *Courtesy of Chip deMatteo*

William G. deMatteo's record card for his #49 Danish tea service. *Courtesy of Chip deMatteo*

Another example of DeMatteo's original designs in the Jensen style is his no. 251 oval centerpiece. No real corollary exists in the Georg Jensen A/S of Copenhagen catalogs for this piece, but it is unmistakably Jensenesque. It proved so popular that Georg Jensen Inc.'s New York store continued to sell it long after 1945, featuring it in their advertising and displaying it in their window.

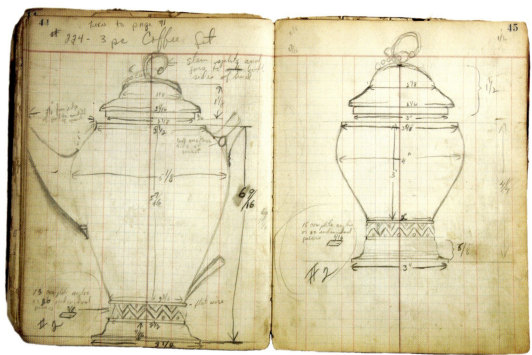

William G. deMatteo's design records book, pages 44 and 45. Left, "#224- 3 pc Coffee Set" with zig-zag foot. Right, "15 complete angles or 30 individual pieces." *Courtesy of Chip deMatteo*

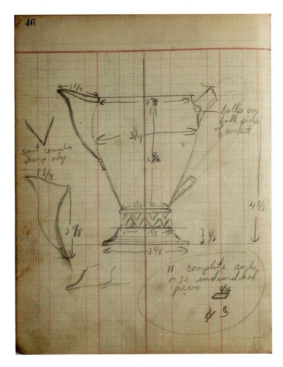

William G. deMatteo's design records book, pages 46 and 47. Left, "spout comes to sharp edge. Balls on both sides of socket. 11 complete angles or 22 individual pieces." *Courtesy of Chip deMatteo*

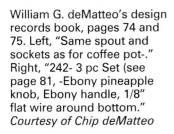

William G. deMatteo's design records book, pages 74 and 75. Left, "Same spout and sockets as for coffee pot-." Right, "242- 3 pc Set (see page 81, -Ebony pineapple knob, Ebony handle, 1/8" flat wire around bottom." *Courtesy of Chip deMatteo*

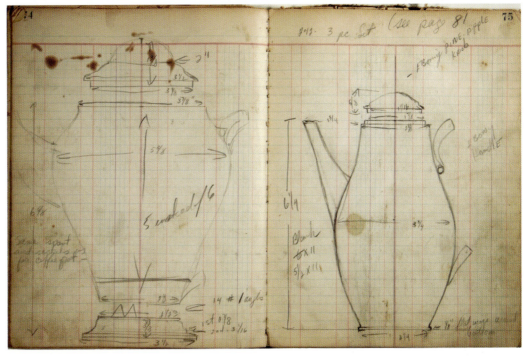

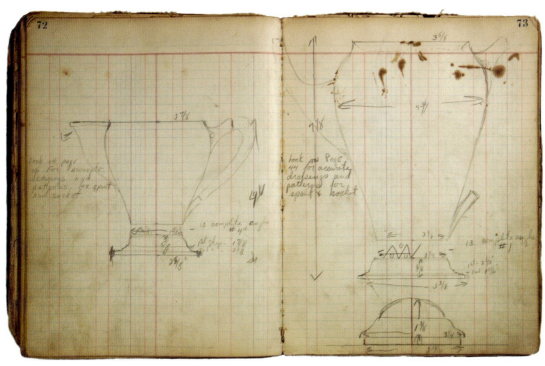

Below: William G. deMatteo's design records book, pages 74 and 75. Left, "Same spout and svockets as for coffee pot-." Right, "242- 3 pc Set (see page 81, -Ebony pineapple knob, Ebony handle, 1/8" flat wire around bottom." *Courtesy of Chip deMatteo*

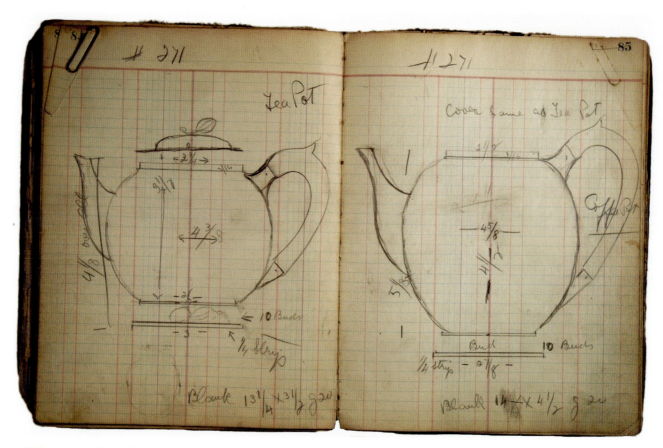

William G. deMatteo's design records book, pages 84 and 85. Left, "# 271, Tea Pot, 10 buds, ¼ Strips, Blank 13 ¼ x3 ½ g20." Right, "#271, Coffee Pot, Cover Same as Tea Pot, 10 Buds, ¼ strip, Blank 14 x 4 ½ g20." *Courtesy of Chip deMatteo*

William G. deMatteo's design for #399 Coffee Pot. *Courtesy of Chip deMatteo*

Covered sugar bowl, a flaring vase, and a cream pitcher made by William G. deMatteo. *Courtesy of Chip deMatteo*

A triangular bowl with a lid and a serving spoon, both made by William G. deMatteo, 5" high. *Courtesy of Chip deMatteo*

Small footed bowl made by William G. deMatteo, 4 ½" high.
Courtesy of Chip deMatteo

Medium-sized footed bowl made by William G. deMatteo.
Courtesy of Chip deMatteo

Small footed bowl made by William G. deMatteo, 4 ½" diameter
x 4 ½" high. *Courtesy of Chip deMatteo*

Small round bowl with zig-zag base made by William G.
deMatteo, 4 ½" diameter x 4" high. *Courtesy of Chip deMatteo*

Large bowl with a beaded rim, grape clusters, and flower buds decorating the raised base, made by William G. deMatteo, 14" diameter x 7" high. *Courtesy of Chip deMatteo*

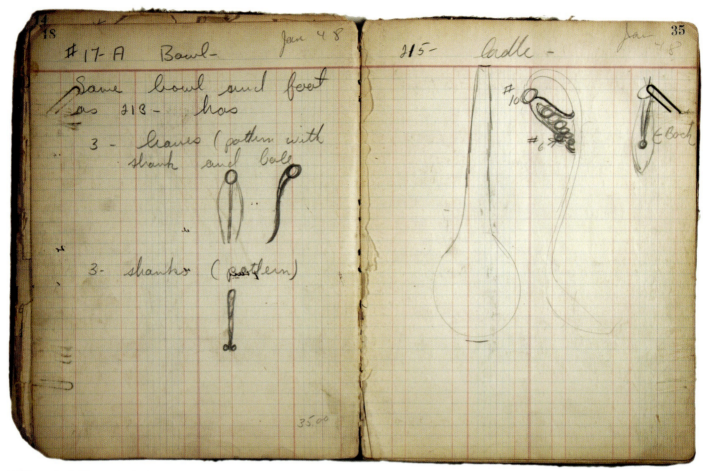

William G. deMatteo's design records book, pages 18 and 35. Left, dated January 1948. Design "#17-A Bowl- Same bowl and foot as 221B- has 3- leaves (pattern with shank and ball. 3- shanks (pattern). Right, dated January 1948. Design "215- ladle-. *Courtesy of Chip deMatteo*

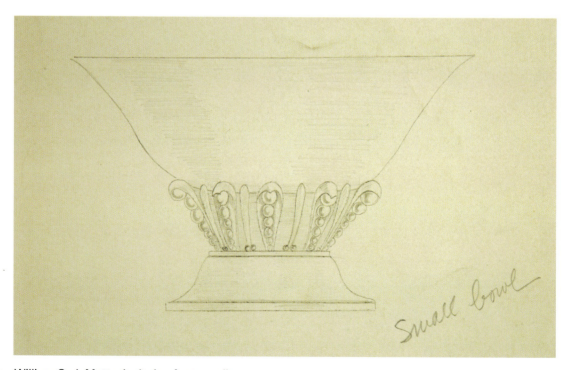

William G. deMatteo's design for a small bowl. *Courtesy of Chip deMatteo*

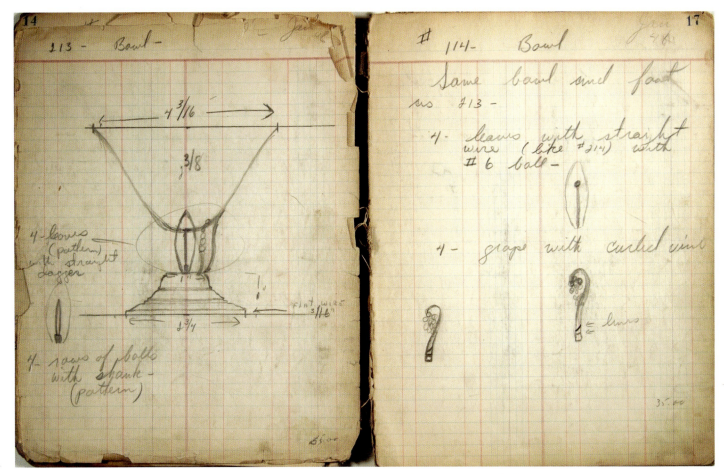

William G. deMatteo's design records book, pages 16 and 17, Left page with design for #213 bowl.
Right page with design for "#114- Bowl. Same bowl and foot as no 213 – 4- leaves with straight
wire (like #214) with #6 ball- 4- grape with curled vine." *Courtesy of Chip deMatteo*

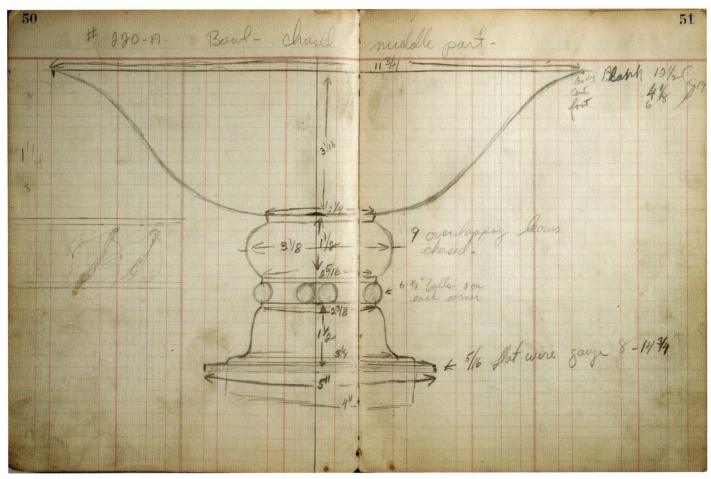

William G. deMatteo's design records book, pages 50 and 51. Left, "#220A- Bowl- chased." Right,
"middle part-. Body Blank 12 ½ (g 19), center 4 1/8, foot 6. 9 overlapping leaves chased-. 6- 3/"
balls 2 on each corner. 5/15 flat wire gauge 8- 14 ¾." *Courtesy of Chip deMatteo*

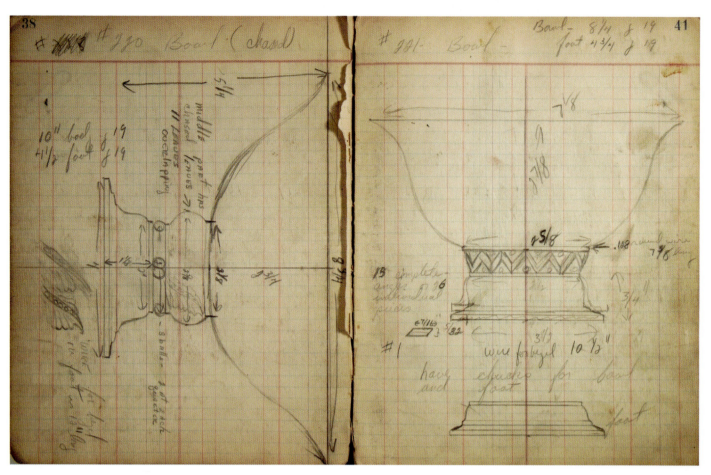

William G. deMatteo's design records book, pages 38 and 41. Left, "#220 Bowl (chased) Middle part has chased leaves, 11 leaves overlapping." Right, "#221-Bowl." Zig-zag pattern in the foot. *Courtesy of Chip deMatteo*

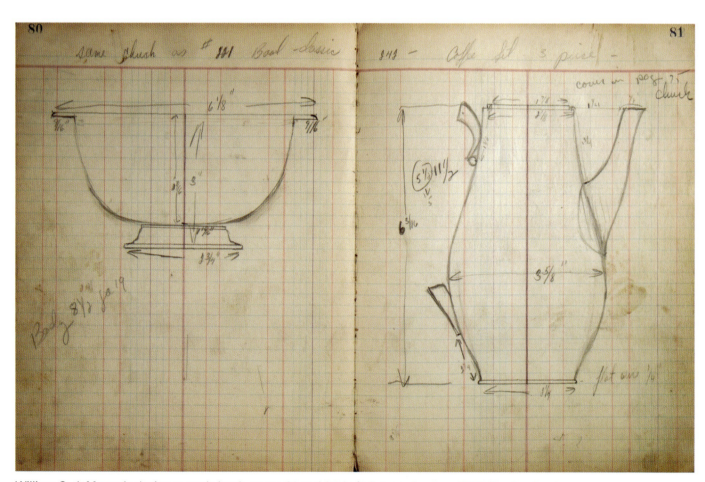

William G. deMatteo's design records book, pages 80 and 81. Left, "same chuck as #221 Bowl – classic, Body 8 ½" ga19." Right, "242- Coffee Set. 3 piece-, cover on page 75, chuck, flat wire ¼"." *Courtesy of Chip deMatteo*

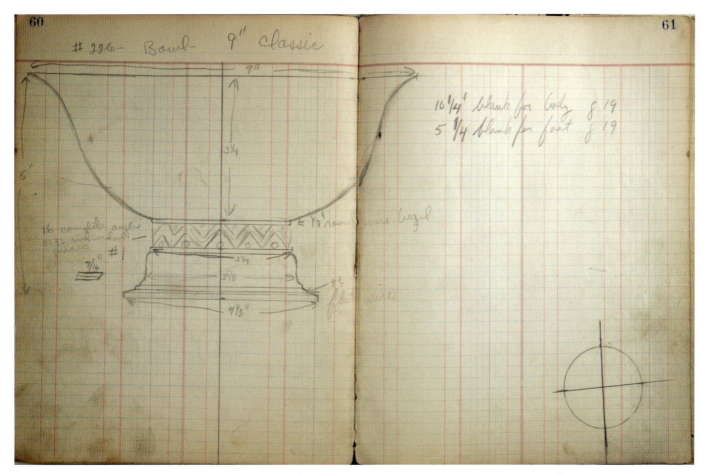

William G. deMatteo's design records book, pages 60 and 61. Left, "#226- Bowl- 9" classic, [zig-zag pattern of] 26 complete angles or 32 individual pieces, 1/8" round wire bezel, 7" flat wire." Right, "1/4" blank for body g19, ¼["] blank for foot g19." *Courtesy of Chip deMatteo*

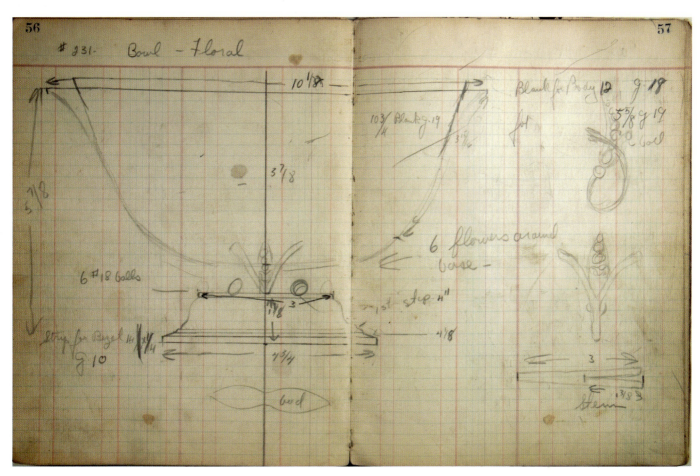

William G. deMatteo's design records book, pages 56 and 57. Left, "#231- Bowl- Floral, 6 #18 Balls, strip for Bezel g10." Right, "Blank for Body 12 g18, 6 flowers around base." *Courtesy of Chip deMatteo*

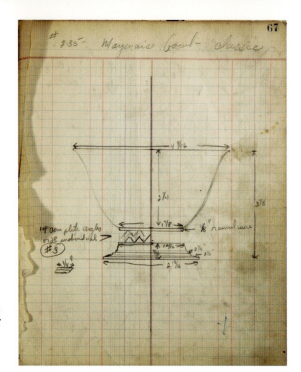

William G. deMatteo's design records book, page 67. "#235-Mayonaise bowl- classic, [zig-zag pattern of] 14 complete angles or 28 individual, 1/8" round wire." *Courtesy of Chip deMatteo*

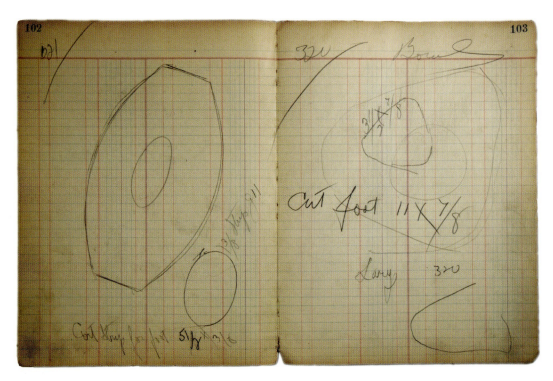

William G. deMatteo's design records book, pages 102 and 103. Left, "321, 3/8" strip g11, Cut Strip for foot 5 ½ x 3/8." Right, 320 Bowl, Cut foot 11 x 7/8, Large 320." *Courtesy of Chip deMatteo*

Large match box by William G. deMatteo, 3" long x 2" wide. *Courtesy of Chip deMatteo*

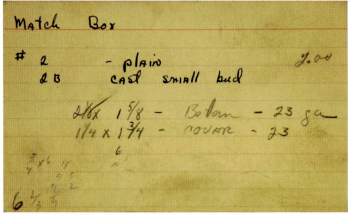

William G. deMatteo's record card for Match Boxes #2 and #2B. *Courtesy of Chip deMatteo*

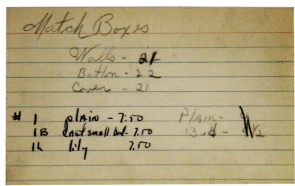

William G. deMatteo's record card for Match Boxes. *Courtesy of Chip deMatteo*

Match box with open striking area and lily top by William G. deMatteo. *Courtesy of Chip deMatteo*

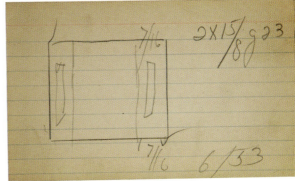

William G. deMatteo's record card with a drawing for match boxes. *Courtesy of Chip deMatteo*

Cigarette boxes made by William G. deMatteo

Rectangular box with hinged top and bud finial by William G. deMatteo. *Courtesy of Chip deMatteo*

Rectangular box with a hinged lid and bud finial made by William G. deMatteo, 5" long x 3" wide. *Courtesy of Chip deMatteo*

Rectangular box with a hinged lid, made
by William G. deMatteo, 5" long x 3" wide.
Courtesy of Chip deMatteo

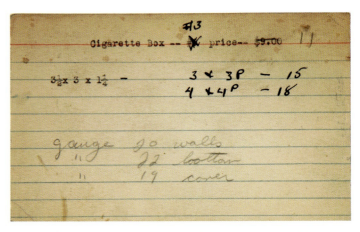

William G. deMatteo's record card for #2 Regular Size
Cig[arette] Box, dated 6/[19]53. *Courtesy of Chip deMatteo*

William G. deMatteo's record card for Cigarette Box #3.
Courtesy of Chip deMatteo

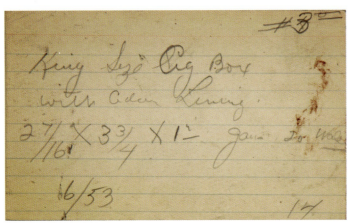

William G. deMatteo's record card for
King Size Cig[arette] Box #3, dated 6/
[19]53. *Courtesy of Chip deMatteo*

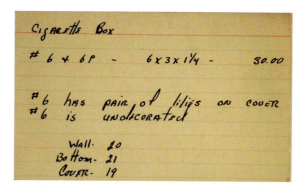

William G. deMatteo's record card for Cigarette Boxes #5 & 5p. *Courtesy of Chip deMatteo*

William G. deMatteo's record card for Cigarette Box #6. *Courtesy of Chip deMatteo*

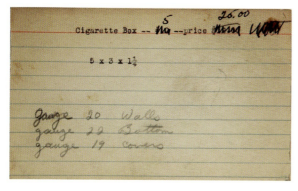

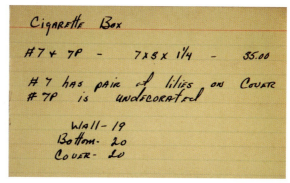

William G. deMatteo's record card for Cigarette Box [#] 5. *Courtesy of Chip deMatteo*

William G. deMatteo's record card for Cigarette Box #7. *Courtesy of Chip deMatteo*

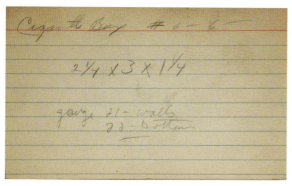

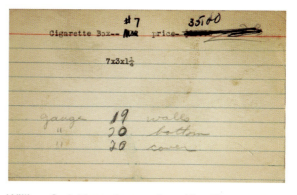

William G. deMatteo's record card for Cigarette Box #6. *Courtesy of Chip deMatteov*

William G. deMatteo's record card for Cigarette Box #7. *Courtesy of Chip deMatteo*

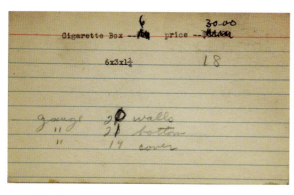

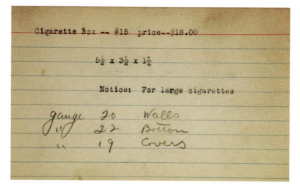

William G. deMatteo's record card for Cigarette Box #6. *Courtesy of Chip deMatteo*

William G. deMatteo's record card for Cigarette Box #15, "For large cigarettes." *Courtesy of Chip deMatteo*

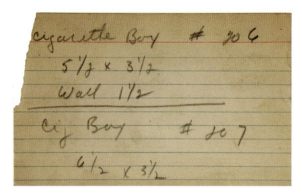

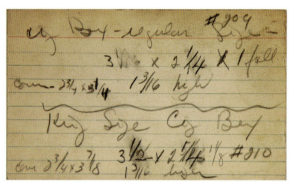

William G. deMatteo's record card for Cigarette Cup #206 and Cig[arette] Box #207. *Courtesy of Chip deMatteo*

William G. deMatteo's record card for Cig[arette] Boxes, regular #209 and King Size Cig[arette] Box #210. *Courtesy of Chip deMatteo*

Oval hinged box with a lilies finial made by William G. deMatteo, 3" diameter x 4" high. *Courtesy of Chip deMatteo*

Small castor by William G. deMatteo, 3 ½" high. *Courtesy of Chip deMatteo*

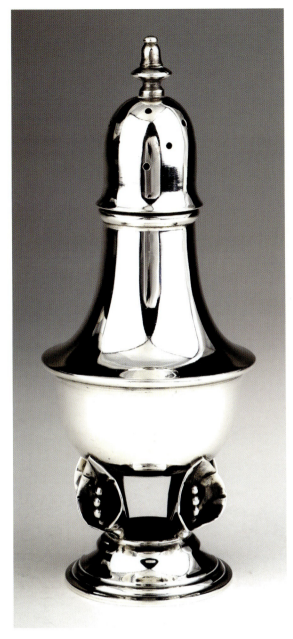

Lily base caster by William G. deMatteo, 6" high.
Courtesy of Chip deMatteo

Zig-zag base caster by William G. deMatteo, 5".
Courtesy of Chip deMatteo

Pair of tall candlesticks
made by William G.
deMatteo, 4" diameter
x 11" high. *Courtesy of
Chip deMatteo*

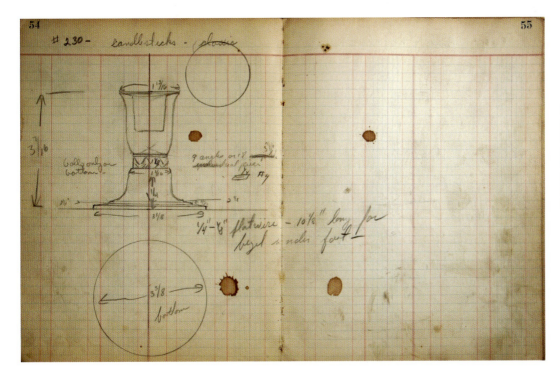

William G. deMatteo's design records book, pages 54 and 55. Left, "#230- candlesticks-classic. Balls only on bottom- 9 angles or 18 individual pieces. Flat wire 10 1/8" long for bezel under foot-." *Courtesy of Chip deMatteo*

William G. deMatteo's design for a 2-arm candlestick. *Courtesy of Chip deMatteo*

William G. deMatteo's design for a single candlestick. *Courtesy of Chip deMatteo*

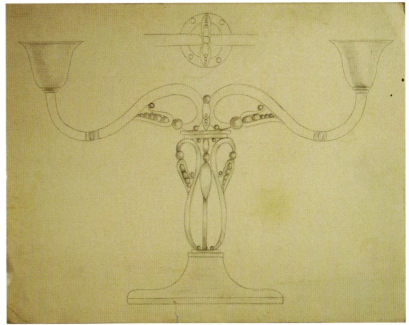

Another of William G. deMatteo's designs for a 2-arm candlestick. *Courtesy of Chip deMatteo*

A pair of 2-light candlesticks with bud ornaments made by William G. deMatteo, 10" wide x 8" high. *Courtesy of Stanley J. Szaro, Lauren Stanley American Silver, New York*

A round ashtray with a
cigarette rest made by
William G. deMatteo,
4" diameter. *Courtesy
of Chip deMatteo*

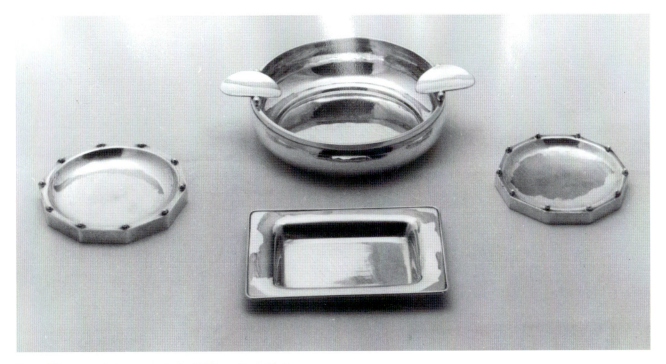

Four different ash trays made by William G. deMatteo

A cigarette stand made by William G. deMatteo, 3" high. *Courtesy of Chip deMatteo*

A small and a large cocktail shaker made by William G. deMatteo. *Courtesy of Chip deMatteo*

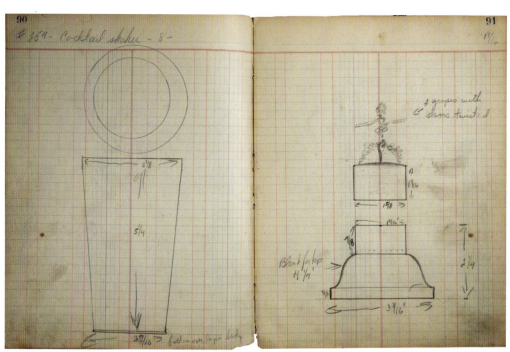

William G. deMatteo's design records book, pages 90 and 91. Left, "#254- Cocktail shaker-8-, bottom overlaps body." Right, "2 grapes with stems twisted, Blank for top 4 ¼"." *Courtesy of Chip deMatteo*

Compote of helix shape with grapes, made by William G. deMatteo, 7" diameter x 7" high. *Courtesy of Chip deMatteo*. See also Chapter 3 for a comparison of compote designs.

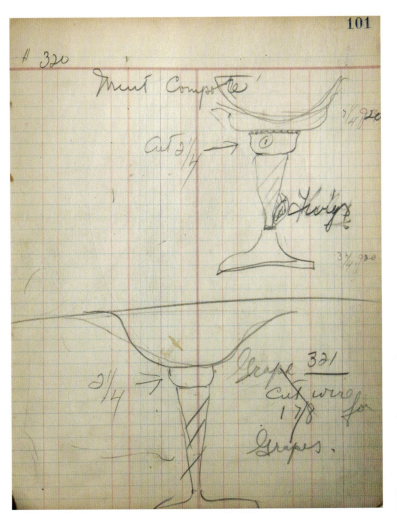

William G. deMatteo's design records book, page 101. #320 Mint Compote, cut 2 ¼→. Twigs. [#]321 [Compote] Grape, cut wire for Grapes." *Courtesy of Chip deMatteo*

Compote of helix shape with lilies ornaments, made by William G. deMatteo, 7" high. *Courtesy of Chip deMatteo*

Glass condiment pot with silver lid and serving spoon by William G. deMatteo, 4 ½" high. *Courtesy of Chip deMatteo*

Julep cup with zig-zag base by William G. deMatteo, 6" high. *Courtesy of Chip deMatteo*

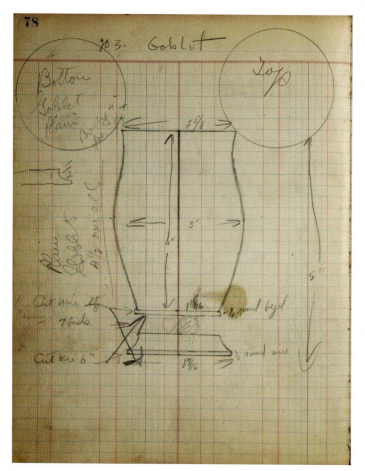

William G. deMatteo's design records book, page 78. "203- Goblet, Bottom Goblet Plain, Cut Wire, 7 buds, Cut Wire, Top, ½ round bezel, ½ round wire." *Courtesy of Chip deMatteo*

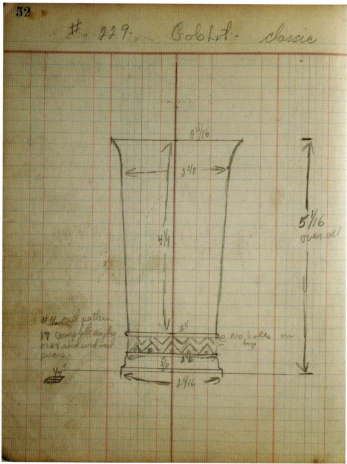

William G. deMatteo's design records book, page 52 "# 229 Goblet- classic. #4- cast pattern, 17 complete angles or 34 individual pieces- no balls on top." *Courtesy of Chip deMatteo*

Small shot cup with a hexagonal beaded base by William G. deMatteo, 3" diameter. *Courtesy of Chip deMatteo*

Julep cup with a base decorated with flower buds by William G. deMatteo, 6" high. *Courtesy of Chip deMatteo*

Baby cup by William G. deMatteo, 2 ½" diameter x 3" high. *Courtesy of Chip deMatteo*

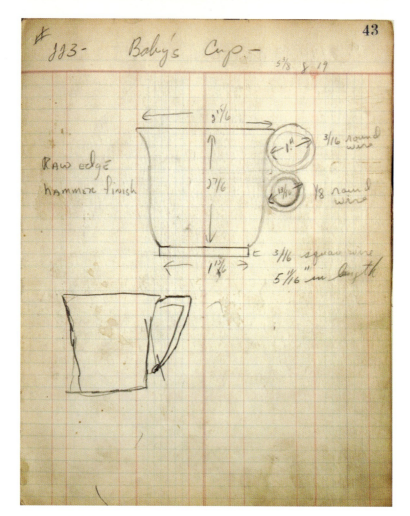

William G. deMatteo's design records book, page 43. "#223-Baby's Cup." *Courtesy ofv Chip deMatteo*

Shallow round bowl with buds around the foot, made by William G. deMatteo, 6" diameter x 2" high. *Courtesy of Chip deMatteo*

A boat-shaped dish with a base, made by William G. deMatteo, 11" long x 3 ½" high. *Courtesy of Chip deMatteo*

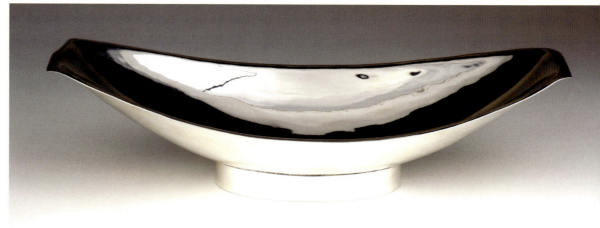

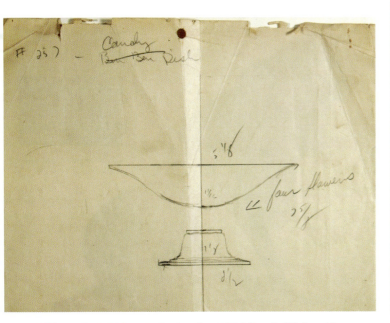

William G. deMatteo's design for #257 Candy Dish, with four flowers, after 1949. *Courtesy of Chip deMatteo*

The back of the #257 Candy Dish drawing by William G. deMatteo, using a calendar page from November, 1949, as his drawing paper. *Courtesy of Chip deMatteo*

A two-leaf candy dish made by William G. deMatteo. *Courtesy of Chip deMatteo*

A single-leaf candy dish made by William G. deMatteo, 8" long, *Courtesy of Chip deMatteo*

Gravy boat #253
made by Wiliam
G. deMatteo.
*Courtesy of Chip
deMatteo*

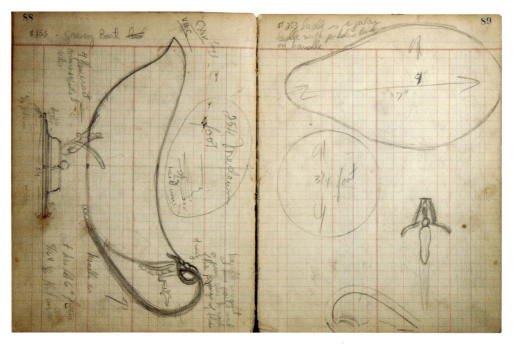

William G. deMatteo's design records book, pages 88 and 89. Left, "#253 – Gravy Boat.
4 flowers at rims & 4 balls at sides, double strip, 5/16" flat wire. 254 Medium foot, wire,
handle is split at this point and a prong goes to each of the prongs of the twig." Right,
"#253 ladle is regular ladle with podalin (?) bud on handle, 3 ¼ foot." *Courtesy of Chip
deMatteo*

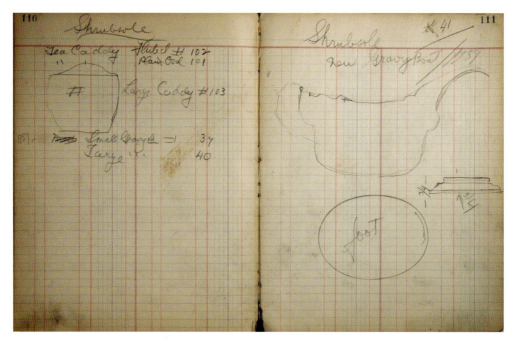

William G. deMatteo's design records book, pages 110 and 111. Left, Shrubsole, Tea Caddy,
Fluted #102, Plain bowl [#]101. Large Caddy #103. Small Gravy (?) B= 39, Large [ditto]
40." Right, "Shrubsole #41 New Gravy Boat / 1959, foot." *Courtesy of Chip deMatteo*

A Danish-style footed cup and a pitcher with lilies decoration, both made by William G. deMatteo. *Courtesy of Chip deMatteo*

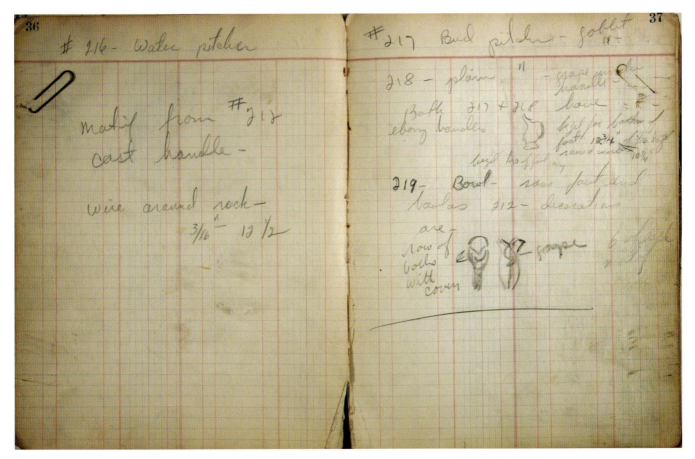

William G. deMatteo's design records book, pages 36 and 37. Left, "#216- Water pitcher. Motif from #218, cast handle 4- wire around neck-." Right, "#217 Bud pitcher – goblet. 218- plain. Both 217 and 218 have ebony handle. 219- Bowl- same foot and bowl as 212- decorations are [left] row of balls with cover, [right] –grape." *Courtesy of Chip deMatteo*

Zig-zag salt cellar with a cobalt glass insert and a spoon, both made by William G. deMatteo, 3" high. *Courtesy of Chip deMatteo*

Lily-base salt cellar with a cobalt glass insert and a spoon, both made by William G. deMatteo, 3" high. *Courtesy of Chip deMatteo*

William G. deMatteo's design records book, pages 58 and 59. Left, "#232- Pepper Shaker-classic, cast knob (pattern), holes- Divide into 8-, balls only on bottom, classic design, #7- 8 complete angles or 16 individual pieces. Right, #233 – Open Salt- (classic), glass liner- 7/8" deep, 2 ¼" in diameter, 8 complete angles or 16 individual pieces, balls only on bottom." *Courtesy of Chip deMatteo*

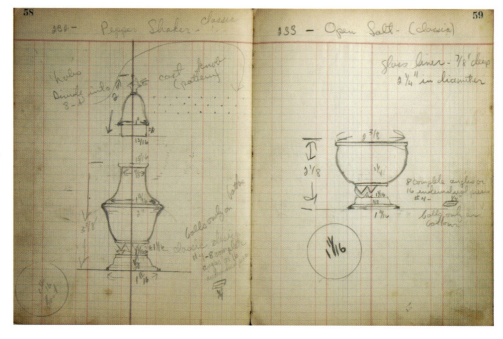

William G. deMatteo's design records book, pages 96 and 97. Left, "Blank, Compotes Lip 7 ¼ g.19, foot 3 ¾ g.20. Blank for Covered Compote #318, Body 3/8 g19. Foot 3xg.20. Cover 2 ¼ g.21." Right, "Pepper & Salt 107." *Courtesy of Chip deMatteo*

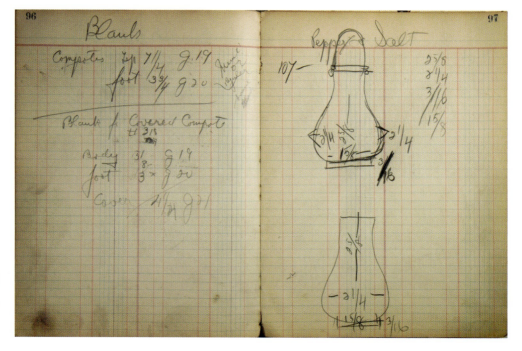

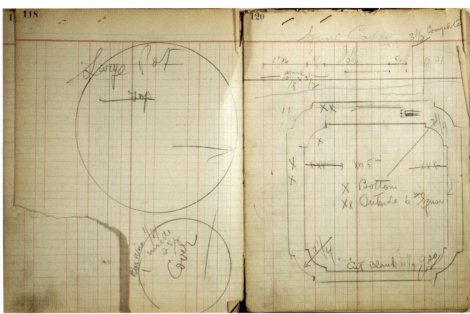

William G. deMatteo's design records book, pages 118 and 120. Left, "Large Pot, Top. Cut Wire ¼ inside 2 5/8 Cover." Right, "Square Caddy, 3 ½ Complete. J.R. Bottom Outside 6 in. Square. Cut Blank 6 ½ g20." *Courtesy of Chip deMatteo*

A small 10-sided tray with beads, made by William G. deMatteo, 3 ½" diameter. *Courtesy of Chip deMatteo*

A tea caddy with a flat lid and flame finial, made by William G. deMatteo, 3" diameter x 4 ½" high. *Courtesy of Chip deMatteo*

William G. deMatteo's design records book, pages 70 and 71. Left, "#239- 14" Scroll bordered waiter- 8 sections- order blank. 239F- feet. #240- 14: thread bordered 8 sections, 240F footed. 241- 14" plain scalloped waiter 8 sections, 241F footed." Right, "#224- 4pc classic. [zig-zag of] 15 complete angles of #3- large balls on bottom." *Courtesy of Chip deMatteo*

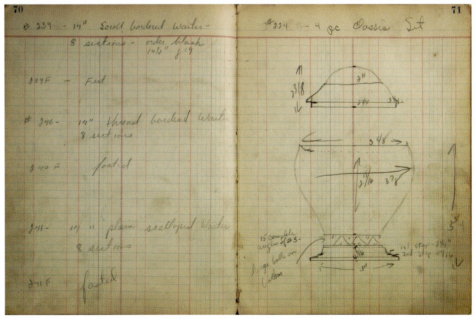

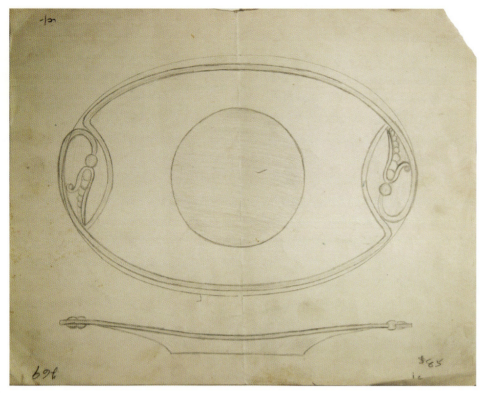

William G. deMatteo's design for #269 tray. *Courtesy of Chip deMatteo*

Oar-shaped shoehorn made by William G. deMatteo. *Courtesy of Chip deMatteo*

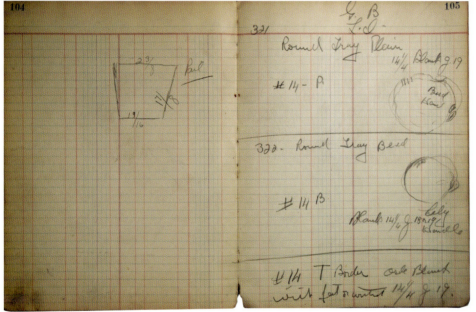

William G. deMatteo's design records book, pages 104 and 105. Left, "Pail." Right Top, "321 G. B. L. I., Round Tray Plain, Blank g19. #14-P, Bud Handle (?)." Right Center, "322- Round Tray Bead #14B, Blank 14 ¼ g18 or 19 Handle." Right Bottom, "#14 T Border Orde Blunt, with feet or without 14 ¼ g19." *Courtesy of Chip deMatteo*

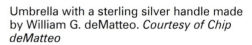

Umbrella with a sterling silver handle made by William G. deMatteo. *Courtesy of Chip deMatteo*

Small pail with a twisted handle made by William G. deMatteo, 3 ½" diameter. *Courtesy of Chip deMatteo*

Pair of salad serving spoons with large buds on the handles, made by William G. deMatteo, 10" long. *Courtesy of Chip deMatteo*

Serving spoon with a bud on the handle, made by William G. deMatteo, 9" long. *Courtesy of Chip deMatteo*

Gravy ladle with a leaf on the handle, made by William G. deMatteo, 6" long. *Courtesy of Chip deMatteo*

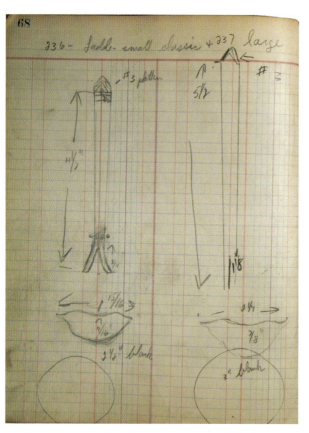

William G. deMatteo's design records book, page 68, "#236- Ladle- small classic + 237 large." *Courtesy of Chip deMatteo*

Gravy ladle with a bud on the handle, made by William G. deMatteo, 6" long. *Courtesy of Chip deMatteo*

Large ladle with grapes detail, made by William G. deMatteo, 12" long. *Courtesy of Chip deMatteo*

A flat server with a large
bud on the handle, made by
William G. deMatteo, 9" long.
Courtesy of Chip deMatteo

A flat, forked server with a
lily on the handle, made by
William G. deMatteo, 10" long.
Courtesy of Chip deMatteo

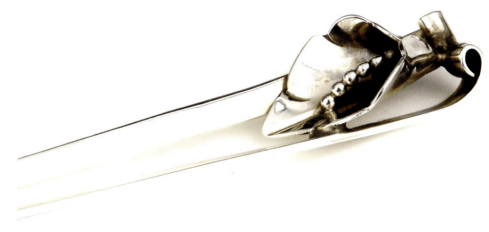

If the modern styles declined in popularity in his private business, deMatteo supplemented them with early American reproductions. He continued to mark the items he made with a capital D in a circle or with the capital letters DEMATTEO (see page 13). He retired from his own silversmith company in New Jersey in 1967, but later would produce items that he was commissioned to make by his son Bill.

After his time in the Navy, William G. deMatteo's son, William L. "Bill" deMatteo (1923-1988), became a professional silversmith. It was he who demonstrated his craft for many years as the Master Silversmith for the Colonial Williamsburg Foundation in Williamsburg, Virginia. When William G. deMatteo retired from his main business in New Jersey in 1967, he worked with his son part of the time in Virginia. There they made many styles of early American reproductions. In 1968, William G. deMatteo retired to Florida and left his many tools, including those he had used to make items for Georg Jensen Inc., and many of his silver pieces to his family. The deMatteo family is proud of his work and his measure of quality – "O.K. for Fifth Avenue." Bill deMatteo marked the silver items he made throughout his career with his last name, "deMatteo," in a rectangle.

Bill deMatteo gained international fame from his private commissions and his work in Williamsburg, and his talent was recognized by the American Institute of Architects that awarded him its Gold Medal. Among his many commissions, he made a bell for Winston Churchill, reproduction Paul Revere lanterns for the Oval Office in the White House during John F. Kennedy's presidency, and a tea service for Queen Elizabeth of England. In 1975, he was the first American silversmith inducted into the Goldsmiths' Company in London. Bill deMatteo retired from Colonial Williamsburg in 1979 and died in 1988.

A third generation of deMatteo silversmiths continues the profession, as Chip deMatteo (b. 1949) runs Hand and Hammer Silversmiths in Woodbridge, Virginia. Bill deMatteo, Phil Thorp, and Chip deMatteo began this business in 1977 and developed their own line of silver goods. Today they make a wide variety of silver ornaments and jewelry, and mark them with the name of their company, Hand and Hammer Silversmiths.

Silversmith Bill deMatteo with his wife and son, Chip, at Colonial Williamsburg, Virginia, in the 1950s. *Courtesy of Chip deMatteo*

Bill deMatteo in his workshop chasing a silver item, 1976. *Courtesy of Chip deMatteo*

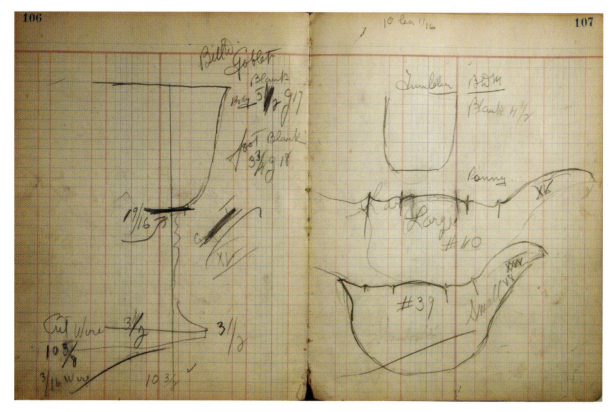

William G. deMatteo's design records book, Pages 106 and 107. Left, Bill D. Goblet, Blank, Body 5 ½ g17, foot Blank 3 ¾ g18, Cut Wire 3 ½. 3/16 wire." Right, "Tumbler BDM, Blank 4 ½, Danny, Large #110, #39 Small." *Courtesy of Chip deMatteo*

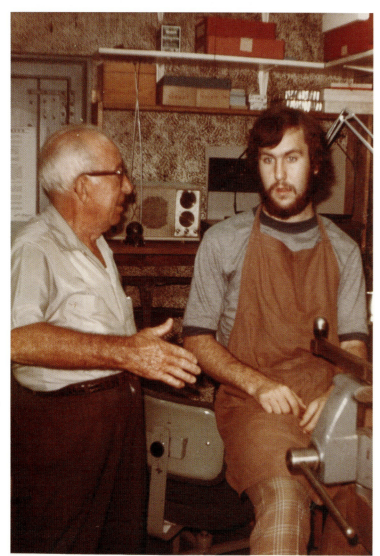

Silversmiths Chip deMatteo and his grandfather, William G. deMatteo, in 1972. *Courtesy of Chip deMatteo*

Silversmith Chip deMatteo in 2007. *Courtesy of Chip deMatteo*

Danish Modern Designs
Become Widespread

The Metropolitan Museum Exhibit, New York, 1960

Georg Jensen silver was among the items shown at a major exhibition called "The Arts of Denmark: Viking to Modern," which was held at The Metropolitan Museum of Art in New York in 1960. Historic items were shown as well as modern pieces from the Georg Jensen workshop in Copenhagen by its major designers. Just Lunning, president of Georg Jensen Inc., chaired the working committee in the United States. This exhibition attracted thousands of visitors and firmly established Danish designs as influential to modern styles.

The Renwick Exhibit, Washington, D.C., 1980

A major exhibition of Georg Jensen silver was held at the Smithsonian Institution's Renwick Gallery in Washington, D. C. in 1980. "Georg Jensen Silversmith: 77 Artists, 75 Years" presented 147 items of the Copenhagen firm's most famous designers and demonstrated their influence on independent silversmiths and companies in the United States. This exhibit attracted thousands of visitors, both American and foreign, and cemented the reputation of Georg Jensen and the Danish modern style in which he worked to a receptive audience throughout the world.

Scandinavian Modern Costume Jewelry and Decorative Arts

Even costume jewelry manufacturers in America, including Danecraft and Coro, produced and sold items with Scandinavian-inspired designs in the 1950s and 1960s. Jewelry, furniture, textiles, and housewares with Nordic-inspired designs have become great favorites internationally, and continue to be available today in retail stores worldwide. Scandinavian style is now firmly part of Western culture in all the decorative arts.

Bibliography

deMatteo, Chip. Interviews and correspondence with the authors, 2006-2007.

Drucker, Janet. *Georg Jensen: A Tradition of Splendid Silver*. Atglen, Pennsylvania: Schiffer Publishing, Ltd., 2001.

Moro, Ginger. "The Mystery Designers For Georg Jensen USA," *Heritage*, *Jewelers' Circular-Keystone*, June, 1996, p. 168.

Rainwater, Dorothy. "Alphonse La Paglia: Silversmith and Designer," *Silver Magazine*, May/June, 1995, p. 8.

Rainwater, Dorothy. *Encyclopedia of American Silver Manufacturers*. Atglen, Pennsylvnia: Schiffer Publishing, Ltd., 1988.

Rosenberg, Alan. "Questions of Originality in the Silver Designs of Alphonse La Paglia," New York: Graduate Studies Symposium, Fashion Institute of Technology, April, 1996.

The Lunning Prize. Stockholm: Nationalmusum, 1986.

Index